THE CIVIL PRACTITIONER'S
GUIDE TO THE HUMAN
RIGHTS ACT 1998

THE CIVIL PRACTITIONER'S
GUIDE TO THE HUMAN
RIGHTS ACT 1998

Wendy Outhwaite, MA(Oxon), Licenciée speciale en droit européen
and
Marina Wheeler, MA(Oxon), Licenciée speciale en droit européen

OLD BAILEY PRESS

LAW IN PRACTICE SERIES

OLD BAILEY PRESS
200 Greyhound Road, London W14 9RY

ISBN 1 85836 336 5

British Library Cataloguing-in-Publication Data

A catalogue record for this book is available from the British Library.

Printed and bound in Great Britain

Contents

Contents

Foreword

From the entry into force of the Human Rights Act 1998, the European Convention and the jurisprudence of the European Court of Human Rights will cease to be the domain of specialists and become part of the stock-in-trade of every legal practitioner in the United Kingdom. The impact of the Act on the various areas of civil practice is explained in this volume with elegance and economy. After setting out the machinery of the Act and identifying the incorporated rights, the authors go on to give a substantive account of the claims it may be possible to frame in each area, on the basis of those rights. The way in which the convention might be deployed on different sides of the same argument (about the switching off of a life-support machine, say, or intrusive reporting by the media) is strikingly brought out. Nor are theoretical issues neglected, such as the interplay between Convention notions and *Wednesbury* unreasonableness. The authors are to be congratulated for making so much clear, while wasting so few words.

Professor A A Dashwood,
Professor of European Law and Director
of the Centre for European Legal Studies,
University of Cambridge

Preface

Many people, and practitioners, assume that 'rights' are the preserve of the criminal law system: the rights of an accused to be informed of the charge against him; the right to be brought before a court promptly after arrest etc. This assumption is false and one which this book is intended to dispel. The Human Rights Act 1998 will affect all areas of law: civil and criminal. It will bring changes to legal techniques such as the interpretation of legislation, as well as altering the substantive law and existing procedural rules. With the recognition of individual rights such as the right to respect for private and family life, or the right to a fair trial, we will see significant changes in the law from personal injury and medical law to family law, from employment to environment law, from land law to public law.

This books offers the civil practitioner a concise guide to the most important legal development since the UK's accession to the Treaty of Rome. Its aim is to help the civil practitioner to recognise, tackle and exploit the human rights points in cases with confidence.

Chapter 1 introduces the Human Rights Act 1998 and provides a brief background to the European Convention on Human Rights. It summarises the main aspects of the HRA as well as how it will operate and whom it will affect.

Chapter 2 looks in more detail at the content of the Convention rights and the legal concepts used by the ECHR in applying the Convention (such as 'proportionality'). It summarises the main application of each important Convention article and highlights the areas of law where they have had the greatest impact to date.

Chapters 3–11 are devoted to illustrating how these rights may alter the substantive law. Each chapter deals with a different area of civil practice and, largely through a digest of the Strasbourg jurisprudence, examines the possible impact of the HRA on each area of practice covering medical and personal injury law, family law, employment law, judicial review, environmental law, land law, civil procedure, privacy and confidentiality and education.

Chapter 12 examines the relationship between the HRA and EC law. It looks at the emergence of EC human rights principles (general principles or fundamental principles of EC law) and identifies the advantages and disadvantages of bringing a claim under the HRA on the one hand and EC law on the other.

Chapter 13 deals with practical aspects of bringing a claim under s6 HRA such as who may claim, how a claim should be pleaded and what the time limits are.

Chapter 14 is concerned with remedies. It sets out the remedies available under the HRA and, in view of the requirement that regard be had to the principles applied by the ECHR in determining damages awards, examples are given of such awards made by the ECHR where possible in cases previously referred to in the text.

The text of the HRA appears as an annex.

The HRA obtained Royal Assent on 9 November 1998 and is currently expected to come into force in the spring of 2000. This delay has been considered necessary to allow the judiciary in particular to prepare. It should be recognised, however, that the HRA has some retrospective effect. After entry into force, a defendant will be able to rely on a Convention right (ie as a defence) in respect of an allegedly unlawful act committed during the transitional period between enactment and entry into force. It is also the case that the devolution provisions of the Northern Ireland Act 1998, the Scotland Act 1998 and the Government of Wales Act 1998 will give effect to Convention rights before the HRA comes into force.

The law, as stated, is correct as at April 1999.

Acknowledgements

The ideas put forward in this book are of course personal and speculative. However, we have benefited and derived assistance from attending a course of seminars in 1998 organised by Justice in conjunction with the Bar at which we were able to exchange ideas with other practitioners interested in the field of human rights.

We would like to thank our colleagues Malcolm Sheehan and Geraint Webb for their drafts of Chapters 8 and 5 respectively. Our thanks also to our clerks in chambers who have been patient and tolerant, particularly when deadlines loomed.

Wendy Outhwaite
Marina Wheeler
April 1999

Table of Cases

1   The Human Rights Act 1998

Curbing state power

On one point the legal profession is united. Legal seminars, practitioners' texts, judges' addresses: all draw the same happy conclusion from their study of the Human Rights Act (HRA) 1998. There will be 'opportunities ahead'. There will be 'interesting times to come'. (And, the cynics might add, there will be fees.) The press, too, is probably right that the HRA will encourage litigation and increase the powers of judges. In applying the HRA, judges will inevitably foray into the political arena and will at times brazenly 'make law'. But that is not the aim of the Act. Its aim, and its likely achievement, will be to impose some express limits on the power of government.

Our present system is based on majority rule, where Parliament is free to do whatever it chooses. Currently public officials acting pursuant to statute (subject to compliance with EC law and the rules of natural justice) are free from admonition. The HRA will constrain such action and require public bodies to respect the rights of individuals as set out in the Convention for the Protection of Human Rights and Fundamental Freedoms (the Convention). In future some rights and freedoms will be deemed so fundamental that they cannot be taken away even by the will of the majority.

By domestic tradition, the citizen is free to do as he likes unless his proposed action is unlawful. Once the Convention is incorporated, the starting point will no longer be this qualified freedom, but the rights which every citizen will enjoy under the Convention. The question will shift from whether the citizen is in the wrong, to whether public authority is in the wrong. As the state continues to grow and to encroach ever more on the lives of citizens, this process has become essential and builds on the development in last 25 years of the judicial review of the decisions of government bodies.

The Convention

The Convention was signed on 4 November 1950 by the founding nations of the Council of Europe, to ensure, through binding rules of conduct, that there could be no repetition of the atrocities of the Second World War.

The UK led the drafting of the Convention, and was its first signatory (there being, now, 39 others). But, unlike the majority of continental signatories, it strongly resisted incorporation into national law. While other countries which did incorporate dealt with human rights' claims domestically, the British citizen wishing to assert a Convention right was forced to petition the European Court of Human Rights (ECHR) in Strasbourg. Not only was this expensive and time-consuming for the applicant, but it led to a vast body of decisions against the UK which gave the it an unjustified reputation as a large-scale abuser of human rights.

Since the late 1960s, the merits of incorporation have been widely discussed. But until it was embraced as a cause by John Smith (then leader of Labour party), in a lecture to Charter 88 on 1 March 1993, it seemed unlikely to occur. In its 1997 White Paper 'Bringing Rights Home', the present government signalled its own commitment to the reform. It has been a long time coming. By the time the HRA comes into force in the spring of 2000, it will be 50 years since the Convention was signed.

The government seems at pains to stress that the HRA does not confer new rights, it just does away with the lengthy trip to Strasbourg. It is presented merely as 'an improved mechanism' to enforce existing Convention rights. That is beguiling. The judiciary is in little doubt that incorporation is a radical step. Lord Woolf has referred to it as 'revolutionising our legal world', and Professor Wade has described incorporation as 'one of our great constitutional milestones'. Certainly it is the most important legal development since the Treaty of Rome.

Although not bound by it, judges have of course relied on the Convention in the past. However, the reality has been that advocates who brought it up were usually considered to have reached a low point in their submissions and were, putting it bluntly, 'scraping the barrel'. Once the HRA comes into force, this will change.

The Human Rights Act

The Act is deservedly praised. Referred to in its early life as 'a very cleverly crafted Bill' (per Lord Donaldson of Lymington) and later as 'an elegant piece of machinery', the HRA, in 22 sections and four schedules, introduces the Convention into English law in a way which is said to satisfy 'both the constitutional purist and, in large measure, the reforming modernist'.

The constitutional purist rails at the Treaty of Rome but will accept the HRA because the principle of parliamentary sovereignty remains intact.

Under the HRA, the domestic courts will have no power to overturn an Act of Parliament which conflicts with a Convention article. In contrast, Community law obliges the domestic courts to set aside statutes which conflict with Community law. Community law is 'supreme': *Administrazione delle Finanze* v *Simmenthal* [1978] ECR 629 and *R* v *Secretary of State for Transport, ex parte Factortame* [1990] ECR 1–2433. If a statute conflicts with the Convention, the best that can be obtained from the courts is a declaration of incompatibility.

Structure and summary of the HRA

Section 1 of the Act selects the following Convention rights for incorporation:

- Articles 2–12 and 14 of the Convention;
- Articles 1–3 of the First Protocol; and
- Articles 1 and 2 of the Sixth Protocol;

as read with arts 16–18 of the Convention.

These rights are set out in Schedule 1 to the Act:

Article 2:	Right to life
Article 3:	Prohibition of torture or inhuman or degrading treatment or punishment
Article 4:	Prohibition of slavery and forced labour
Article 5:	Liberty and security of the person etc
Article 6:	Right to a fair trial
Article 7:	Freedom from retrospective criminal offences and punishment
Article 8:	Right to respect for private and family life
Article 9:	Freedom of religion
Article 10:	Freedom of expression
Article 11:	Freedom of assembly and association
Article 12:	Right to marry and found a family
Article 14:	Prohibition of discrimination in enjoyment of Convention rights
First Protocol:	
Article 1:	Protection of property
Article 2:	Right to education

Article 3:   Right to free elections

Sixth Protocol: Abolition of the death penalty

The notable omissions from this list are arts 1 and 13.

Section 2 of the HRA requires any court or tribunal determining a question which has arisen in connection with a Convention right to take into account the jurisprudence of the ECHR, the Commission of Human Rights (the Commission) and the Committee of Ministers. As of November 1998, these bodies have been amalgamated into a reconstructed ECHR. The term 'take into account' makes it clear that this jurisprudence is not binding but is intended to offer guidance. Domestic courts will be free to use the ECHR jurisprudence as a springboard to develop their own jurisprudence, perhaps affording a higher standard of protection. However, any attempt to draw back from rights guaranteed by the ECHR will be likely lead to a complaint direct to the ECHR.

Sections 3–8, 10, and 19 are devoted to methods of giving effect to the 'incorporated' rights. Broadly speaking, the rights are introduced into English law by three routes:

1. via s3, which provides that legislation (both primary and subordinate) must be read and given effect (so far as is practicable) in a way compatible with Convention rights ('the interpretative route');

2. via ss6–8, which create a new cause of action that together make it unlawful for a public authority to act in a way that contravenes a Convention right (s6), and entitles a person to bring proceedings against such a body if it commits such an act (s7), and specifies the courts' powers to grant a remedy where an act (or proposed act) is found to be unlawful. The definition of a public authority is contained in s6(3), and the definition of who is entitled to complain (ie a 'victim') is found in s7(1);

3. by mechanisms that put pressure on government and Parliament to bring existing and future legislation in line with the Convention, eg a declaration of incompatibility under ss4–5; remedial action under s10; and statements of compatibility under s19.

Interpretation of the Convention pursuant to s3 will require the 'teleological' or purposive approach familiar to practitioners of Community law (see for example the construction in *Lister* v *Forth Dry Dock and Engineering Co* [1990] 1 AC 546 where additional words were 'written in' to ensure the domestic legislation complied with EC law). In contrast to traditional statutory interpretation, whereby the words of a statute are

4

given their plain and natural meaning, the teleological approach requires an enactment to be construed 'in the light of its object and purpose'. A feasible interpretation which is compatible with the Convention will thus prevail even if there is nothing to suggest Parliament intended such a meaning when the statute was enacted. As the following chapters will show, the teleological approach has allowed the meaning of the Convention rights to evolve according to changing social norms. This feature has prompted to ECHR to refer to the Convention as 'a living instrument which ... must be interpreted in the light of present day conditions': *Tyrer* v *UK* (1978) 2 EHRR 1.

Section 11 expressly states that reliance on a Convention right does not restrict any other right or claim. This may mean, for example, that the one-year limitation period under the Act (s7(5)) will not apply if, under a another cause of action raised simultaneously, the period would be longer. For example, if a breach of a Convention right is raised in a personal injury action, the relevant limitation period may remain three years.

The Convention contains no hierarchy of rights. However, as a result of intense lobbying by the media and the churches, the HRA (in ss12 and 13) grants a special status to the Convention articles on freedom of religion and freedom of expression (arts 9 and 10 respectively). Section 12 accordingly restricts the courts' ability to grant relief in the absence of a respondent, and its ability to restrain publication of material before trial in cases which involve the freedom of expression. Such restraint will only be ordered if the applicant can show he will succeed at trial. Further, the court is required to 'have particular regard to the importance of freedom of expression', and if the material under challenge seems to be of a journalistic, literary or artistic nature, the court should have regard to:

1. the extent to which the material has already been published;

2. the public interest in publication; and

3. any relevant privacy code.

Section 13 achieves a similar aim in beefing up the art 9 rights to freedom of religion. It requires that particular regard be had to those rights. The inclusion of these sections is surprising given that there is nothing in the Strasbourg jurisprudence to suggest such rights have been undervalued or need extra reinforcements.

Sections 14–17 preserve the Secretary of State's powers to make reservations and derogations from the Convention and Protocols. To date the UK has made one derogation in respect of art 5(3) of the Convention requiring an arrested person to be brought before a court within a reasonable time. It has also made one reservation in relation to art 2 of the First Protocol on education.

Who will the HRA affect?

The new cause of action under ss6–7 is only enforceable against public authorities (whether in initiating a claim or as a defence in proceedings brought by public bodies). However, it will have a significant, if indirect, impact on relations between private parties (so as to have some 'horizontal effect'). As will be seen in later chapters, some Convention articles impose positive obligations on states to protect individuals against infringement of the rights in question, including infringement by third parties: *X and Y* v *The Netherlands* (1985) 8 EHRR 235.

Beyond this, the HRA will have a major impact on all litigants whether they be private parties or public authorities, by obliging the domestic courts:

1. to decide all cases before them compatibly with Convention rights, unless they are prevented from doing so by primary legislation (or provisions made under primary legislation which cannot be read compatibly with the Convention): s3(1)–(3);

2. to interpret existing and future legislation in conformity with the Convention wherever possible: s3;

3. to take the jurisprudence of the ECHR into account where a Convention question has arisen: s2(1).

What will the HRA change?

The following Chapters 3 – 12 are devoted to answering the question, namely: 'What will this constitutional milestone' actually change? Some possibilities are:

• creation of a right to privacy to challenge media intrusion;

• erosion of the paramountcy principle in Children Act cases;

• loss of local authority immunity from civil suit in areas in which it is currently enjoyed;

• a finding that restrictions on the availability of civil legal aid are sometimes unlawful;

• creation of a right to a clean environment;

• use of the Convention to challenge rationing by the NHS;

• steps to equalise the treatment of unmarried fathers and transsexuals;

- more effective ways for mental patients to challenge their detention;
- more openness in local authority decision-making and greater procedural fairness;
- methods of challenging the conditions in which vulnerable people (old people, children in care and mental patients) are looked after by local authorities.

For the practitioner, caught up in these changes, the first step is to become acquainted with the Convention and the jurisprudence of the ECHR, whilst recognising that many cases turn on their very particular facts.

2 The Incorporated Rights

Introduction

By the standard of modern constitutions, the Convention is not a radical document. It does not protect social or economic rights but promotes the traditional civil and political rights – those necessary for participation in the democratic process – such as the freedom of expression, conscience, religion, assembly, association and rights necessary for a fair trial.

The Convention is a 'living instrument'. The ECHR has used it to evolve the rights of homosexuals, the ban on corporal punishment in English schools and the development of environmental rights.

In its first judgment, *Golder* v *UK* (1975) 1 EHRR 524, the ECHR considered that the right to a fair trial contained in art 6(1) guaranteed a right to access to a court through a lawyer, notwithstanding the lack of express wording. Since then, the ECHR has refused to be bound to a literal approach.

The structure of the rights and Convention concepts

The Convention contains both absolute rights, which do not permit derogation, and qualified rights, which allow justifiable interference in limited circumstances. Articles 2, 3, 4, 7, 12 and 14 contain absolute rights. The qualified rights in arts 8–11 contain common features, both substantive and formal, and are constructed in an identical way: the first paragraph defines the protected right, and the second paragraph sets out the conditions upon which a state may legitimately interfere with the enjoyment of those rights.

Interference with a right is permitted if it is:

1. 'in accordance with the law' or 'prescribed by law'; and
2. 'necessary in a democratic society in the interests of', variously, national security, public safety, for the protection of public order, health or morals, or for the protection of the rights and freedoms of others etc.

'In accordance with the law'

This term is synonymous with the term 'prescribed by law', and means that, as a minimum, a state must identify some specific rule or regime authorising the interference it seeks to justify. The law must be accessible in that individuals must be able to predict the outcome of the application of such law. In other words, the law must be sufficiently precise to allow a person to regulate his conduct. Statutory regulation in not essential, the common law may be adequate, but mere guidelines are insufficient: see especially *Sunday Times* v *UK* (1979) 2 EHRR 245 and *Malone* v *UK* (1984) 7 EHRR 14.

'Legitimate aim'

A defendant must identify the objective of the interference. It will often identify more than one. The ECHR may find that the aim suggested by the state is not the 'real reason' for the interference. However, the aims set out in the Convention are so wide that a state can usually satisfy this requirement and make a case that it had a good reason for the interference.

Not only must the interference be 'in accordance with the law' and pursuant to a legitimate aim but it must also be 'necessary in a democratic society'.

'Necessary in a democratic society'

An interference will only be necessary if it 'corresponds to a pressing social need and is proportionate to the legitimate aim pursued': *Silver* v *UK* (1983) 5 EHRR 344.

Proportionality, put colloquially, is the duty not to use a sledgehammer to crack a nut. As a rule of thumb, a public authority will act proportionately if there is a balance between the aim and the means used to achieve it. If the aim can be achieved in different ways, the public authority must adopt the option that least restricts the protected Convention right. Inherent in this exercise is the need to strike a fair balance between 'the demands of the general interests of the community and the requirement of the protection of the individuals fundamental rights': *Soering* v *UK* (1989) 11 EHRR 439.

In deciding if an interference is 'necessary' in this sense, the ECHR allows the contracting states a 'margin of appreciation'.

'Margin of appreciation'

The margin of appreciation is that discretion left in the states to enforce Convention rights.

In *Handyside* v *UK* (1976) 1 EHRR 737 the ECHR explained:

> '... by reason of their direct and continuous contact with the vital forces of their countries, state authorities are in principle in a better position that the international judge to give an opinion on the exact content of those requirements [of morals] as well as on the "necessity" of a "restriction" or "penalty" intended to meet them ...'

However, the ECHR has made it clear that while it is for the national authorities to make the initial assessment of the strength of the need implied by the notion of 'necessity', this is subject to European supervision. The ECHR will give the final ruling on whether a restriction is reconcilable with a Convention right.

A certain deference is, therefore, shown to the judgment of public authorities in balancing conflicting public and individual interests. However, the more important the right, the more serious the justification must be for the interference.

The margin of appreciation is a Strasbourg concept demanded by considerations of national sovereignty and subsidiarity. It is irrelevant once the Convention is enforced by the domestic courts. English judges should be firmly steered away from attempting to rely on the doctrine (or following ECHR cases which turn on this) so as to avoid determining the lawfulness of an interference with a Convention right.

The incorporated articles

Article 2: The right to life

Article 2 is an absolute right. No derogations are permitted, even in times of war or public emergency. No one may be deprived of his life except in accordance with conditions prescribed by law, defined in art 2(2), to cover, broadly, the use of necessary force in self-defence, to effect an arrest and to quell riots. Defence of property is not an exception. To date only two cases have been decided by the ECHR, although the Commission has considered many more.

The Commission's jurisprudence establishes that art 2 places a negative obligation on states not to take life intentionally, and a positive obligation to protect the right to life by law. Article 2 thus imposes on states the following duties:

- to assist in an emergency (*Hughes* v *UK* (1986) 48 DR 258);
- to warn, monitor and give information if there is a threat to life (*LCB* v *UK* [1998] TLR 381);

- to legislate to make killing illegal (*W v UK* (1983) 32 DR 190);
- to provide adequate and effective measures to prevent killing, such as effective police and security forces;
- to protect its citizens from life-threatening situations such as terrorism (although the degree and adequacy of the protection is left to the state);
- to investigate and prosecute suspicious deaths (killings by agents of the state demand 'public and independent scrutiny' such as a police investigation or inquest (*McCann, Farrell and Savage* v *UK* (1995) 21 EHRR 97); and
- to plan in order to minimise the threat to life, for example when quelling riots (*Gulec v Turkey* (1998) 27 July (unreported) and *McCann, Farrell and Savage* v *UK*).

As noted above, art 2 does not prohibit all killing. The following do not infringe art 2:

- capital punishment, although the Sixth Protocol ensures its abolition;
- killing in self-defence where the force used is no more than absolutely necessary;
- killing in the course of arresting or preventing the escape of a person lawfully detained where the force used is no more than absolutely necessary (*Farrell* v *UK* (1982) 30 DR 96; *Kelly* v *UK* No 17579/90 (1993) (unreported));
- killing in the course of quelling a riot or insurrection where the force used is no more than is absolutely necessary.

To be lawful, force must be necessary and proportionate to the achievement of the permitted purpose: *Stewart* v *UK* (1984) 38 DR 162. In *Gulec* v *Turkey* (above) the security forces shooting into a crowd of demonstrators was disproportionate and unlawful. Armed terrorists or criminals may therefore be shot if such killing is necessary and proportionate, but these terms are strictly applied. In *McCann, Farrell and Savage* v *UK* (above) three IRA members, believed to be about to detonate a car bomb in Gibraltar, were shot dead by the SAS, allegedly when they made sudden movements when approached. The ECHR held the actions of SAS members who shot the terrorists did not violate art 2 but the control and organisation of the operation did.

Article 2 is increasingly invoked in the medical context. Chapter 3 on medical law considers the compatibility of euthanasia and abortion with art 2.

Article 3: Prohibition of torture or inhuman or degrading treatment or punishment

Article 3 is also absolute and echoes the text of the Universal Declaration of Human Rights.

'Torture' is defined as 'deliberate inhuman treatment causing very serious and cruel suffering': *Ireland v UK* (1978) 2 EHRR 25. In the *Greek Case* (12 YB (ECHR) 194 (1969)) torture was defined as an aggravated form of inhuman treatment 'which has a purpose, such as the obtaining of information or confession, or the infliction of punishment'. Mental anguish alone may be torture if it is sufficiently serious.

'Inhuman treatment' must 'attain a minimum level of severity'. An intention to cause suffering is not essential: *Ireland v UK* (above). The threat of torture could be inhuman treatment: *Campbell and Cosans v UK* (1982) 4 EHRR 293. In addition to findings against Greece and Turkey, interrogation methods of the British security forces in Northern Ireland in the 1970s, such as prolonged wall-standing, hooding, subjection to noise, sleep deprivation and reduction in diet, have been found to violate art 3: *Ireland v UK* (above)

Beyond the expected application seen above, the ECHR has creatively interpreted art 3 to condemn corporal punishment, control deportations and regulate medical treatment. In *A v UK* [1998] TLR 578 a stepfather's licence to beat a child with a garden cane causing actual bodily harm if it was 'reasonable chastisement' was held to be inhuman treatment. Deportation and extradition may be inhuman treatment if the deportee is separated from his family (*Berrehab v The Netherlands* (1988) 11 EHRR 322); if there is a disproportionately severe criminal sentence awaiting him (*Soering v UK* (1989) 11 EHRR 439); if the receiving state is unable or unwilling to protect his life (*Chahal v UK* (1996) 23 EHRR 413); or if there is a real risk of ill-treatment because of political persecution: *Vilvarajah v UK* (1991) 14 EHRR 248.

Chapter 3 on medical law looks at the extent to which experimental treatment, a lack of proper treatment and detention of patients in poor conditions may violate art 3.

The following is not inhuman treatment: life imprisonment, even if without the possibility of review (*Kotalla v The Netherlands* (1988) 14 DR 238); insanitary conditions and overcrowding in detention (*B v UK* (1981) 32 DR 5 and *McFeeley v UK* (1981) 3 EHRR 161); solitary confinement (although this will be decided on its facts and 'its effects on the person concerned'): *X v Germany* (1973) 44 CD 115.

Degrading treatment involves such disrespect of human dignity that it 'grossly humiliates': the *Greek Case* (above). An objective test is adopted. A public act is not required. Degrading treatment includes birching (*Tyrer* v *UK* (1978) 2 EHRR 1) and racial discrimination: the *East African Asian Cases* (1973) 3 EHRR 76. However, handcuffing in public, prison uniforms (even prior to conviction) (*Campbell* v *UK* (1992) 15 EHRR 137) and the non-recognition of a transsexual's new sex (*B* v *France* [1992] FLR 249) are not degrading.

Article 4: Prohibition of slavery and forced labour

Applications under art 4 are rare. Applications arise in respect of convicted prisoners and the obligation on professionals to provide services to the community

Freedom from slavery and servitude

No derogation is permissible.

'Slavery' (according to the 1926 Slavery Convention) is 'the status or condition of a person over whom any or all of the powers attaching to the right of ownership are exercised'. 'Servitude' is the obligation to provide services and live on another's property without the 'serf' being able to change his condition: *Van Droogenbroeck* v *Belgium* (1982) 4 EHRR 443.

Freedom from forced or compulsory labour

A pupil lawyer's obligation to provide free legal services was not forced labour as it was proportionate to the benefit acquired (that is, the future practice of the legal profession) and so was deemed to be voluntarily undertaken: *Van der Mussele* v *Belgium* (1983) 6 EHRR 163. For further discussion see Chapter 5.

The state must legislate against forced or compulsory labour.

The following is not 'forced or compulsory labour':

1. work required to be done while in detention, including work on convicts, minors and vagrants (*X* v *Switzerland* (1979) 18 DR 238);
2. military or civilian service (whether compulsory or voluntary) for conscientious objectors;
3. community service in a public emergency, for example, public dental service (*Iversen* v *Norway* 6 YB 278 (1963)); and
4. normal civil obligations, such as calculating an employee's tax.

Article 5: The right to liberty and security of the person

Article 5 prevents the arbitrary deprivation of liberty. The right to liberty and security of the person is qualified, but art 5 details procedural safeguards, in the event of detention or arrest, which must be respected.

A person may be deprived of his liberty:

1. after conviction by a court;
2. for contempt of court;
3. on remand for commission of a crime;
4. detention of a minor for educational purposes;
5. inter alia, the compulsory admission of patients to a mental hospital; and
6. inter alia, of illegal immigrants and those who it is determined should be deported or extradited.

Derogation from art 5 is possible in an emergency.

A person deprived of his liberty must be:

1. informed promptly and in a language he understands of the reasons for his arrest and the nature of the charges against him;
2. able to challenge speedily the lawfulness of his detention and obtain his release if unlawful (the habeus corpus provision);
3. be brought promptly before a judge if on remand and be tried within a reasonable time.

Article 5 has been applied mainly in the criminal context. Habeus corpus proceedings have recently been held to satisfy art 5.

In civil cases art 5 is important to the detention of mental patients (see Chapter 3 on medical law), and is also invoked in the context of deportations and extradition. Detention conditions fall under art 3.

The deprivation of liberty must be 'in accordance with a procedure prescribed by law'. It must not be arbitrary. The ECHR will, therefore, scrutinise restrictions on the right to liberty for proportionality in the same way it deals with rights relating to arts 8–11. The degree of scrutiny varies. As seen in Chapter 3 on medical law, the ECHR will analyse medical evidence to assess the decision to detain a mental patient (*Winterwerp* v *The Netherlands* (1979) 2 EHRR 387), but will not question a conviction resulting in imprisonment. Similarly, the ECHR will require that deportation proceedings are taken with 'requisite diligence', but will not examine the merits: *Kolompar* v *Belgium* (1992) 16 EHRR 197.

This is the only article which explicitly requires domestic compensation. The state may fix the level of award but compensation must not be so minimal as to render the right unenforceable: *Tara Cumber* v *UK* No 28779/95 (1997) (unreported).

Article 6: The right to a fair trial

Article 6(1) protects the right to a fair trial in civil and criminal proceedings. Article 6(2) establishes the presumption of innocence in criminal proceedings and art 6(3) sets out minimum rights for those charged with criminal offences. This book is concerned with art 6(1).

The civil limb of art 6(1) applies not just to conventional court proceedings but to any 'determination of ... civil rights and obligations' which covers all proceedings which are decisive for private rights and obligations' (*Ringeisen* v *Austria* (1971) 1 EHRR 455) irrespective of how a state categorises them. For example, it covers an administrative decision which affects the legal relationship between private individuals. It also covers a right to engage in commercial activity and the right to liberty under art 5, but does not cover immigration cases or the right to state education. In *Geoffrey and Margaret Robins* v *UK* (1997) 26 EHRR 527 the Court found that this article applies to cost proceedings following litigation concerning civil rights. The dispute, which must have a basis in substantive domestic law, may refer not only to the actual existence of a right but also to its scope and manner of exercise.

Fairness of a trial is judged as a whole and states have greater latitude in dealing with civil as opposed to criminal cases. The concept of fairness includes:

- 'equality of arms': each party must have a reasonable opportunity of presenting his case under conditions that do not place him at a substantial disadvantage in relation to his opponent;
- a public hearing and judgment: the judgment must be publicly available, even if not given in open court;
- a reasoned decision: the judgment must be sufficiently clear so that the accused can exercise the right of appeal.
- a hearing within a reasonable time;
- an independent and impartial tribunal: the tribunal must be independent of the executive and of the parties. It must have jurisdiction to examine all questions of fact and law relevant to the dispute before it.

The ECHR has found that art 6, impliedly, also protects the following:

1. Right of access to court – this right must be effective although it is not absolute. No right to appeal is implied.

2. Right against self-incrimination: *Saunders* v *UK* (1996) 23 EHRR 313.

Chapter 9 on civil procedure considers the requirements of art 6 in greater detail.

Article 7: The freedom from retroactive criminal offences and punishment

Article 7 mostly concerns criminal offences and is outside the scope of this book. In any event, it has generated little case law and is rarely breached.

Article 7 does not apply to civil judgments, but it may apply to disciplinary offences: *Engel* v *The Netherlands* (1976) 1 EHRR 647. It probably covers 'regulatory' offences such as civil contempt. In *Harman* v *UK* (1984) 38 DR 53 the applicant solicitor was found guilty of contempt because she allowed a journalist access to documents copied to her under the discovery rules in litigation. The application was admitted for consideration under art 7, it being assumed that civil contempt was 'criminal'.

Article 7 applies when new legislation or the novel interpretation of existing legislation has retroactive effect. However, clarification of the elements of an existing offence will not breach art 7 (*Whitehouse* v *Lemon* (the *Gay News* case) [1979] AC 617; *Handyside* v *UK* (1976) 1 EHRR 737; and see also *R* v *R* [1991] 4 All ER 481 (HL) where it was held that a husband could be criminally liable for raping his wife).

Article 8: Right to respect for private and family life

Article 8 protects private life, family life, home and correspondence.

It imposes the negative obligations on the state not to interference with individuals (the right to be left alone). It also imposes a positive obligation to provide rights for individuals and to protect people against the actions of others which interfere with their art 8 rights. For example, in the transsexual cases (see Chapter 4 on family law) the state did not interfere by preventing treatment to achieve a change of sex. The applicants complained that the state failed to respect their rights (breaching its positive obligation) by refusing to amend their birth certificates.

The ECHR has deliberately avoided defining the scope of art 8 (or the specific interests it protects), leaving it free to develop the case law.

The protected interests

The notion of 'private life' extends beyond privacy. It implies more than 'an inner circle' in which the individual may live his own personal life as he chooses' but comprises also the right 'to establish and develop relationships with other human beings': *Niemietz* v *Germany* (1992) 16 EHRR 97. It covers the 'physical and moral integrity of the person', including his or her sexual life (*X and Y* v *The Netherlands* (1985) 8 EHRR 252), and the capacity of a person to determine his identity: to decide what he wants to be and exercise choice over his name, his style of dress, his sexual identity: *Gaskin* v *UK* (1989) 12 EHRR 36.

As will be seen in later chapters, respect for private life may be violated if the state fails to protect individuals against severe pollution or fails to issue warnings about its impact; and if it fails to provide safeguards against intrusions such as telephone tapping.

The concept of 'family life' is looked at in some detail in Chapter 4 on family law.

Apart from care and contact cases, art 8 is also invoked in immigration and deportation cases by family members who do not have an independent right of residence in the state where the remainder of their family live. Where an applicant has been settled in the state and enjoyed family life there for some time, the right to its continued enjoyment will be strong: see, for example, *Berrehab* v *The Netherlands* (1988) 11 EHRR 322; *Moustaquim* v *Belgium* (1991) 13 EHRR 802; *Beldjoudi* v *France* (1992) 14 EHRR 801; and *Abdulaziz* v *UK* (1985) 7 EHRR 471.

The right to respect for correspondence is a right to uninterrupted and uncensored communication with others. Most ECHR cases concern prisoners' correspondence, especially that of detained persons with lawyers: *Campbell* v *UK* (1992) 15 EHRR 137. It overlaps with respect for private life in that it is expected that correspondence between say, a lawyer and client, or doctor and patient will be private and any interference violates respect for private life. Respect for correspondence aims to protect the means of communication, rather than its content.

Respect for a person's home embraces a right of access and occupation of one's home and a right not to be expelled or evicted from it (accordingly it overlaps with art 1 of the First Protocol: *Buckley* v *UK* (1996) 23 EHRR 191). It regulates intrusion by authorities to arrest, search, seize and inspect. Recently, the ECHR has extended this interest to protect against personal harassment and pollution. This is looked at in some detail in Chapter 7 on environmental law.

Interference and justification

The applicant must establish an interference, and the state must identify a legitimate objective and justification for the interference.

Most cases will turn on whether the interference was 'necessary in a democratic society'. However, an interference must also be 'in accordance with the law' as has been examined most notably in secret surveillance cases, care cases and interference with correspondence. In *Malone* v *UK* (1984) 7 EHRR 14 the ECHR found that the regulation of phone-tapping by administrative practice violated this provision. The UK therefore enacted the Interception of Communications Act 1985. The inadequacy of

UK prison law (an amalgam of statute, delegated legislation, and administrative order) has led to similar changes: *Silver v UK* (1983) 5 EHRR 344.

Some art 8 interests are given greater protection than others, for example the private enjoyment of sexual relations and the rights of prisoners to correspond with legal advisers: *Dudgeon v UK* (1981) 4 EHRR 149; *McComb v UK* (1986) 50 DR 81; and *Campbell v UK* (1992) 15 EHRR 137. The ECHR also places greater importance on certain interests which the state seeks to protect. For example, surveillance made in the interests of national security will generally be accepted as a justification for interference: *Klass v Germany* (1978) 2 EHRR 214 and *Leander v Sweden* (1987) 9 EHRR 43. Whereas more usual interferences which occur in the course of enforcing the criminal law may not: see *Funke v France* (1993) 16 EHRR 297.

The following chapters on family law (Chapter 4), privacy and confidentiality (Chapter 10), and environment law (Chapter 7) all examine these issues further.

Article 9: Freedom of religion

Few claims are brought under art 9, and fewer have succeeded. It protects religious and non-religious beliefs: *Arrowsmith v UK* (1978) 19 DR 5. It includes the right to believe and the freedom to manifest one's belief.

Article 9 overlaps and conflicts with other Convention articles. If an activity is both a manifestation of a belief and an exercise of freedom of expression, art 9 will offer greater protection than art 10: the permitted grounds of interference under art 9(2) are more narrow. Other articles may afford more precise protection than art 9, for example art 2 of the First Protocol requires children to be educated in accordance with their parents' religious or philosophical convictions. In *Hoffmann v Austria* (1994) 17 EHRR 293, a custody dispute between a Jehovah's witness mother and her children fell within art 8, not art 9.

In *Otto-Preminger-Institut v Austria* (1994) 19 EHRR 34 a film considered likely to offend the Catholic majority in a region of Austria where it was likely to be shown was siezed. Surprisingly, the ECHR permitted the interference with the right to free expression as being necessary to protect the religious rights and freedoms of others. This contrasts with *Choudhury v UK* (1991) 12 HRLJ 172 where the lack of criminal sanctions against publications which offended the beliefs of non-Christians did not violate art 9.

Public policy will be reviewed by the ECHR, even if it is based on religious considerations. For example, when the Irish Supreme Court upheld the criminalisation of male homosexuality on a religious basis, the ECHR still found that the right to respect for private life was violated.

The state cannot interfere with an activity because it is a manifestation of religion or belief. However, if the general law incidentally prohibits or restricts such a manifestation, art 9 will not necessarily be breached. In *X* v *UK* (1981) 22 DR 27 the education authority's decision not to release a Moslem teacher to attend prayers during school hours was found to have duly considered his art 9 rights. Similarly, a requirement that all motorcyclists, including turban-wearing Sikhs, wear crash-helmets was held to be permissible to protect public safety.

However, the outcome may be different depending on disruption to state and impact on applicant. In *Prais* v *EC Council* Case 130/75 [1976] 2 CMLR 708, an ECJ case, the applicant Jew successfully complained that holding examinations on a Saturday for a weekday job violated her rights.

Finally, art 9 does not protect conscientious objectors who refuse to comply with the law.

Article 10: Freedom of expression

Article 10 is 'one of the essential foundations of a democratic society, one of the basic conditions for its progress and for the development of every man': *Handyside* v *UK* (1976) 1 EHRR 737. Furthermore, the right to free expression applies both to 'information' or 'ideas' that are inoffensive or favourably received and to those that offend, shock or disturb. Such are the demands of pluralism, tolerance and broad-mindedness without which there is no democratic society.

The ECHR places the greatest importance on protecting political expression (followed in descending order by artistic and commercial expression). Much of the ECHR's jurisprudence under art 10 concerns questions of press freedom. The ECHR perceives the role of the press as a 'public watchdog': see *The Observer and The Guardian* v *UK* (1992) 14 EHRR 153. It stated:

> '... it is incumbent on it to impart information and ideas on political issues just as on these other areas of public interest. Not only does the press have the task of imparting such information and ideas: the public also has a right to receive them.'

The ECHR accordingly uses art 10 to protect the press against intrusion and permit it to perform 'its essential public functions' by, for example, defending its right to protect its sources (see Chapter 10).

In spite of its importance, however, art 10 is subject to more grounds of limitation than any other Convention right. Article 10(2) sets out these grounds:

1. national security or public safety;
2. the prevention of disorder or crime;
3. the protection of health or morals;
4. the protection of reputation or the rights of others;
5. for preventing disclosure of information received in confidence; and
6. for maintaining the authority and impartiality of the judiciary.

Most of these limitations are looked at in Chapter 10. Contempt of court, however, warrants a brief mention.

The *Thalidomide* case (*Sunday Times v UK* (1979) 2 EHRR 245) established that the English law of contempt of court was compatible in principle with art 10(2) as it maintains the authority and impartiality of the judiciary and protects of litigants in so far as it:

1. outlaws attempts to influence the settlement of pending proceedings; and
2. prohibits the publication of material which prejudge the issues in pending litigation.

On the facts of that case the ECHR found injunctions against the *Sunday Times* to violate art 10. Relevant factors were that the articles in question were 'couched in moderate terms' and did not just present one side of the evidence; the 'thalidomide disaster was a matter of undisputed public concern and the families of the victims had a vital interest in knowing all the underlying facts'. In reaching its conclusion, the ECHR emphasised that the courts could not 'operate in a vacuum': while they were the forum for settling disputes, this did not mean that there could be no prior discussion elsewhere.

This was a highly unusual case. Most restrictions on reporting during litigation fall within this permitted justification, particularly when they are found to be consistent with the fair trial requirements of art 6. For example in *Channel Four v UK* (1989) 61 DR 285, the Commission readily accepted a prohibition on broadcasting a contemporaneous reconstruction of a well known criminal appeal on television in order to protect the right to a fair trial ('the rights of others') and the reputation of the court ('the authority and impartiality of the judiciary'). See also *Worm v Austria* (1998) 25 EHRR 454, where an article proclaiming the guilt of the former

Vice-Chancellor and Minister of Finance while awaiting the verdict in his trial for tax evasion was legitimately restrained.

The ECHR also closely guards the right of free speech during election campaigns: see *Bowman* v *UK* (1998) 26 EHRR 1 where the ECHR found the prosecution of a director of the Society for the Protection of the Unborn Child to breach her right to freedom of expression.

Where expression is intended to undermine the democratic process it will not be protected. Accordingly, the Commission has upheld broadcasting bans on members of political parties supporting terrorist groups such as the IRA: see also *Arrowsmith* v *UK* (1978) 19 DR 5. The Commission, however, has been divided over cases involving German civil servants who lost their jobs when their political views were considered incompatible with their contractual obligations to respect the constitution: *Kosiek* v *FRG* (1986) 9 EHRR 328 and *Glassenapp* v *FRG* (1986) 9 EHRR 25.

Article 11: Freedom of assembly and association

These freedoms both aim to protect the right for people to join together to advance their common interests.

- Freedom of peaceful assembly: art 11 protects peaceful gatherings but incidental disruption will not remove art 11 protection. A meeting planned to cause disturbance will not be protected by art 11. States are afforded a wide margin of appreciation in regulating public meetings and marches due to the threat to public order they can pose. Requirements of notification or permission will not normally be interferences, but an outright ban will have to be justified under art 11(2).

- Association: an individual has no right to join a particular association, but equally he cannot be compelled to become a member or be disadvantaged if he chooses not to (the 'negative' freedom of association). The Convention notion of association does not cover professional associations established by law and requiring the membership of all practising professionals. It may include political parties. There is no right to associate for an illegal purpose, but there is probably a right to campaign to change the law.

The right to form and join trade unions is of course a sub-division of the freedom of association and is looked at in some detail in Chapter 5 on employment law. Once an association is set up (be it a trade union or some other association), the state's duty to regulate the ensuing private relationships so as to ensure enjoyment of art 11 rights is subject to a considerable margin of appreciation.

Article 11 has also been invoked to support the right of Druids to celebrate the summer solstice at Stonehenge: *Chappell* v *UK* (1988) 10 EHRR 510. Turkey was recently found to be in violation of it by its act of dissolving the Socialist Party.

Article 12: The right to marry and found a family

Article 12 sets out a narrow right which is widely regulated by the contracting states. The ECHR's jurisprudence has not expanded its scope significantly.

Matters such as form and capacity to marry are governed by national law and are legitimate provided they do not rob the right of its entire content. In a number of cases, the imposition of delays on people's ability to marry has been found to breach art 12: *Hamer* v *UK* (1979) 24 DR 5; *Draper* v *UK* (1980) 24 DR 72; and *F* v *Switzerland* [1987] A 128. In the UK, for example, such findings led to the Marriage Act 1983 allowing prisoners to be married in prison.

There is no duty on contracting states to allow polygamous marriages or marriages according to particular religious ceremonies. The recognition of foreign marriages arises under art 8 not art 12.

Article 12 establishes a right to marry without the intention to procreate, but there is no right to found a family in the absence of a marriage: *Rees* v *UK* (1987) 9 EHRR 56. Where an unmarried couple have a family they are to some extent protected under art 8.

Neither transsexuals nor homosexuals have any right to marry under art 12: '... the right to marry guaranteed by art 12 refers to the traditional marriage between persons of opposite biological sex ...': *Rees* v *UK*. Although some states permit marriage between transsexuals, the court confirmed its *Rees* judgment in *Cossey* v *UK* (1991) 13 EHRR 622. There is also no right to divorce: *Johnston* v *Ireland* (1986) 9 EHRR 203.

The state does not have any duty to provide a system of adoption, but where one exists the conditions on the rights of couples to adopt will be governed by art 12. The Convention's (and the ECHR's) role in regulating IVF treatment and the availability of such treatment to married persons is yet to be clarified. According to the ECHR's jurisprudence limiting the scope of art 12, single people appear to have no remedy where the right to found a family depends on adoption or treatment such as IVF.

These matters are looked at further on Chapter 3.

Article 14: Prohibition of discrimination in enjoyment of Convention rights

This article does not provide a universal bar on discrimination thereby guaranteeing 'equal treatment'. It attaches itself, like a parasite, to other Convention rights. The potential grounds of discrimination are very wide-ranging, particularly the term 'or other status'. Article 14 is 'an integral part of each of the articles laying down rights and freedoms whatever their nature': *National Union of Belgian Police v Belgium* (1975) 1 EHRR 578. It prohibits both direct and indirect discrimination.

'Discrimination' is different treatment but only in analogous situations: see *Lithgow v UK* (1986) 8 EHRR 329. The burden of proving the similarity of the situation is on the applicant: see *Fredin v Sweden* (1991) 13 EHRR 784. This may be a difficult to satisfy.

Theoretically, art 14 may be breached even if the 'host' Convention right is not violated, although the evidential benefit of an actual breach of a Convention right is obvious. Unfortunately, if the host right is breached, the ECHR often does not find a determination on art 14 necessary: see *Dudgeon v UK* (1981) 4 EHRR 149.

Article 14 has been breached in the following circumstances: where a school has discriminatory entrance requirements *(Belgian Linguistic Case (No 2)* (1968) 1 EHRR 252); and where immigration rules preventing a bride or groom who has not yet met his intended spouse from entering the country in order to marry affected mainly Indians with arranged marriages: see *Abdulaziz v UK* (1985) 7 EHRR 471.

Discrimination which does not pursue a legitimate aim and which is not proportionate will be unlawful: see *Belgian Linguistic Case (No 2)* (above).

Articles 16–18 (these regulate the application of other Convention rights)

Article 16 empowers the state to restrict the political activities of aliens (that is, a non-EU citizen) notwithstanding his Convention rights.

Article 17 prevents an individual manipulating the system by relying on Convention rights in order to undermine the Convention. It follows that the state may act against extremists, such as the German Communist Party (*KPD v Germany* 1 YB 222 (1957)) and terrorists and racists: *Glimmerveen and Hagenback v The Netherlands* (1979) 18 DR 187 and *Kuhnen v Germany* (1988) 56 DR 205.

Article 18 prevents the permitted exceptions in the Convention from being used for an improper purpose. It may be breached even if no other article is violated. Proving bad faith, or collusion or an abuse of power is difficult: *Handyside* v *UK* (1976) 1 EHRR 737 and *McFeeley* v *UK* (1981) 3 EHRR 161.

The First Protocol

Article 1

Article 1(1) grants to 'every natural and legal person' the right to the 'peaceful enjoyment of his possessions'. Although the article states that 'no one shall be deprived of his possessions' this is subject to heavy qualification which permits interference:

- 'in the public interest and subject to condition provided by law'; and/or
- to control the use of property in the general interest; and/or
- to secure the payment of taxes or other penalties.

'Possessions' covers a wide range of proprietorial interests, including patents and shares, debts and contractual rights to property such as leases. The Convention protects existing possessions, but not the right to take possession of something new. Anything which entitles the owner to real economic benefit is a 'possession'. However, the mere expectation of a benefit is insufficient.

These distinctions can be fine. For example, is a pension or social security entitlement a possession? The Commission appears to have established that a contributory scheme which creates an individual share in a fund is a possession. However, a non-contributory scheme, where the link between payments (via the general tax system) and the benefit is less clear, is not a possession: *X* v *The Netherlands* (1971) 38 CD 9 and *Muller* v *Austria* (1975) 3 DR 25.

Interference with possessions which affect the economic value of the property is prohibited. Interference with the aesthetic aspects of property (eg by nuisance) is protected elsewhere in the Convention (see Chapter 7).

The article comprises three elements: the peaceful enjoyment of property; the deprivation of possessions; and control of use in the general interest. Recently the ECHR has not distinguished between these elements but instead has tended to assess interference under a single 'fair balance' test, weighing the protection of the individuals rights against the public interest. Article 1 imposes positive obligations on the state to protect the enjoyment of possessions, but the ECHR has not defined the precise extent of such obligations.

The use of this article in land disputes is examined in Chapter 8 and is also referred to in Chapter 7. It has also been invoked by applicants complaining that orders requiring the forfeiture of their goods violate the Convention. In *Handyside* v *UK* (1976) 1 EHRR 737 there was no violation where obscene publications were seized and destroyed. In *Air Canada* v *UK* (1995) 20 EHRR 150 seizure of the applicant's plane used by others to smuggle cannabis, and which the applicant had to pay £50,000 to retrieve, was also considered by the ECHR to be proportionate.

Article 2

The right to education, and the duty to respect the religious and philosophical convictions of parents is accepted 'only insofar as it is compatible with the provision of efficient instruction and training, and the avoidance of unreasonable public expenditure.'

(See Chapter 11 on education.)

Article 3

This protects the right to free elections to the legislature. It comprises a right to vote and a right to stand for election: *Matthieu-Mohin* v *Belgium* (1987) 10 EHRR 1. Conditions may be imposed if pursuing a legitimate aim and if proprtionate: convicted prisoners may be disenfranchised (*H* v *The Netherlands* (1983) 33 DR 242), as may overseas residents: *X* v *UK* (1979) 15 DR 137.

It does not protect any particular system of voting. A challenge to the UK's system of 'first past the post' was inadmissible: *Liberal Party* v *UK* (1980) 21 DR 211.

Compulsion to vote is not prohibited by art 3.

Protocol 6

The death penalty has recently been abolished as required by arts 1 and 2.

3 Medical Law and Personal Injury

A new cause of action

Any breach of an article of the Convention by a public authority is itself actionable. A plaintiff may bring an action against a 'public authority' (see page 111 for definition of public authority), including NHS trusts, for failing to respect his Convention rights. As a private patient's doctor is probably not a 'public authority', an NHS patient will be able to bring an action for the violation of his Convention rights, but a private patient will probably not.

An individual will succeed against a public authority if his Convention rights have been breached, even if there has been no negligence or other breach of duty. The impact on medical negligence litigation is likely to be dramatic. Medical and personal injury litigation will probably be affected most by arts 2, 3, 6(1), 8 and 14 of the Convention.

The wording of certain applicable articles of the Convention, notably arts 2 and 3, is in absolute terms, and therefore a defence of lack of resources for breaching the Convention will probably not succeed. It follows that a NHS trust may no longer have an unfettered discretion to allocate limited resources, as it currently has, following the Court of Appeal's decision in *R* v *Cambridge District Health Authority, ex parte B* [1995] 1 FLR 1056. Instead, the court is likely to adopt the approach of Laws J at first instance where the defendant had to fund treatment which would prolong life, even if life would be prolonged for only a few months, and even if the treatment had only a small chance of succeeding.

This chapter applies equally to all patients, but mental patients merit special and separate consideration.

The obligation to provide medical treatment

Life-threatening conditions

Prevention
The state and public authorities are obliged under art 2 of the Convention to protect and safeguard a person's health from life-threatening conditions: *X* v *UK* (1978) 14 DR 31. This obligation may include a positive duty to

undertake vaccination and screening programmes. The current regional disparities in screening programmes, particularly in respect of cancers and other life-threatening conditions, will need to be resolved.

Treatment

As public authorities are duty-bound to protect life they may be obliged to provide a particular sort of life-saving treatment, arguably whatever the prospect of success and whatever the cost (see above). There may also be a general duty to assist in life-threatening situations, such as medical emergencies, pursuant to art 2 of the Convention. It follows that doctors must intervene to protect life. As a rule, the current discretion not to intervene because, in the assessment of a doctor, it is in the patient's best interests to abstain is likely to disappear. Put simply, if the life can be saved, efforts must be made to do so.

However (surprisingly, given the absolute nature of art 2 of the Convention), preventable deaths do not inevitably violate the Convention. The Convention does not prohibit passive euthanasia. In *Widmar* v *Switzerland* No 20527/92 (unreported) passive euthanasia (where no positive steps are taken to preserve life, and as a result the individual dies) did not violate art 2. In contrast, it is thought that active euthanasia, where the individual dies as a result of a positive act, is likely to violate art 2. The disconnection of a life-support machine arguably may be classified as an act (and therefore unlawful) or, alternatively, an omission to treat (and therefore lawful). It is unclear whether a patient in a persistent vegetative state (PVS) lawfully may be allowed to die by the removal of life-support machinery as in *Airedale NHS Trust* v *Bland* [1993] 1 All ER 821. Interestingly, in that case Lord Lester QC argued that art 8 of the Convention imposed a duty to respect the dignity and moral integrity of a patient in PVS or coma by giving weight to the previously expressed wish to be allowed to die.

The application of art 2 (so far) only extends to living individuals and not to embryos. Abortion is not prohibited by the Convention if the mother's own health is at risk (*Paton* v *UK* (1980) 19 DR 244) or if there is 'a difficult situation of life: *H* v *Norway* No 17004/90 (1992) (unreported). However, 'in certain circumstances', albeit unidentified, the ECHR has indicated that art 2 of the Convention may protect the life of the unborn. If so, the implications for the practice of genetic engineering, embryology and biotechnology are serious. The duty to protect life does not extend to ensuring future life so that sterilisation does not violate the Convention.

The quality of the treatment given

The duty to preserve life may require that more experienced staff (for example, a consultant) be provided where treatment is required for a life-threatening condition.

Further, in *Tanko v Finland* No 23634/94 (1994) (unreported) it was held that 'lack of proper medical care in a case where someone is suffering from a serious illness could in certain circumstances amount to [torture or inhuman and degrading] treatment contrary to art 3' of the Convention. If followed, a public authority must provide 'proper medical care' or risk litigation. Such duty is not limited to cases where there is a risk of death, as is the duty under art 2 of the Convention. The implications are dramatic. For example, art 3 may require the use of an effective, if costly, drug (such as beta-interferon) rather than a less effective but a less expensive one.

If pursued to its logical conclusion, art 3 of the Convention has a potentially revolutionary effect on medical negligence cases. The *Bolam* test (*Bolam v Friern Hospital Management Committee* [1957] 1 WLR 582), which in its diluted form is the duty to take such reasonable care as is identified by a body of respectable medical opinion and which is reasonable, logical and responsible (*Bolitho v City and Hackney Health Authority* [1997] 3 WLR 1152), may be circumvented. The standard would be, simply, whether there was proper care. A finding of medical negligence or breach of duty would be unnecessary: medical care which is not negligent may still be inadequate and found to constitute an actionable breach of the Convention.

Obligation to provide particular facilities

Sometimes a Convention right might be argued in order to prevent the withdrawal of specified facilities. In *R v North and East Devon Health Authority, ex parte Coughlan* [1998] New Law Digest 14 December the applicant, a tetraplegic, had been accommodated in 'Mardon House' which she had been assured was a 'home for life'. The local authority tried to close it. The closure was prevented. Although the case was decided on other grounds, the argument put forward under art 8 (which protects home life) was considered. Such a propostion may respectably be put forward in the future.

Obligation to provide particular treatment

Article 12 of the Convention provides that 'men and women of marriageable age have a right to ... found a family'. Following *R* v *Human Fertilisation and Embrology Authority, ex parte Blood* [1997] 2 All ER 687, it is arguable that a refusal to provide fertilisation treatment violates art 12 and that an authority must provide fertility treatment. Perhaps it might even be relied upon to obtain impotence drugs, such as Viagra, for those wishing to conceive. The positive duty under the HRA to act in a manner which is compatible with the Convention will be noted. The duty is not limited to refraining from an act which is in breach of the Convention.

Experimental and non-consensual medical treatment

Experimental medical treatment is defined as treatment which has not yet been properly established. Such treatment may amount to torture in breach of art 3 of the Convention if there is no consent: *X* v *Denmark* (1983) 32 DR 282. Consent is vitiated if the patient does not know of the experimental nature of the treatment. It is suggested that the patient should at least be told the purpose of the research, the potential benefit, the foreseeable risks and discomfort, the length of time involved and that the patient should be able to withdraw from treatment without sanction or detriment. Similarly, non-consensual treatment may be torture or inhuman and degrading treatment. If the patient has the capacity to consent to treatment, but withholds consent, any treatment without consent risks being torture or inhuman and degrading treatment. Domestic law also prevents non-consensual treatment: *St George's Healthcare NHS Trust* v *S (No 2)* [1998] TLR 299.

Obligation to provide information and warnings

Article 2 of the Convention imposes a duty on public authorities to safeguard life by giving adequate and appropriate information and warnings about threats to life. Failure to do so is an actionable breach. The lack of reliable information available to the public relating to BSE and beef consumption from the Department of Health or relating to contamination of blood plasma with HIV virus might be examples of actionable breaches of the Convention. The standard is not that of reasonable care but rather the adequacy of the protection of the information or warning. Again, lack of resources to finance such warnings or supply of information would probably not provide an effective defence.

In *LCB* v *UK* [1998] TLR 381 the ECHR considered that, if it was known that the applicant's father had suffered excessive radiation exposure, such that there might be a harmful effect on any children, the UK had a duty under art 2 of the Convention to advise the parents in respect of the risks.

A public authority also has a duty to provide an individual with personal information. In *McGinley and Egan* v *UK* [1998] TLR 379 the UK failed to give the applicants' medical records concerning their participation in the Christmas Island nuclear weapons tests. The applicants could not therefore persuade the pension appeal tribunal that their current health problems were caused by radiation exposure. The ECHR held that the failure without good cause to disclose records proving the applicants' claim would undoubtedly constitute a breach of art 6(1).

Obligation to give medical treatment without discrimination

A decision to give medical treatment must not be discriminatory, otherwise art 14 of the Convention, in conjunction with art 2, may be violated. For example, life-saving treatment must not be denied an elderly patient on the ground of his age. This would be unlawful discrimination.

Confidentiality

Medical practitioners have always been under a duty not to disseminate confidential information. However, art 8 of the Convention which protects private and family life makes a breach of such confidences actionable: *MS* v *Sweden* (1997) 3 BHRC 248. The ECHR considers that:

'The protection of personal data, not least medical data, is of fundamental importance to a person's enjoyment of his or her right to respect for private and family life as guaranteed by Article 8 of the Convention. Respecting the confidentiality of health data is a vital principle in the legal systems of all the Contracting Parties to the Convention. It is crucial not only to respect the sense of privacy of a patient but also to preserve his or her confidence in the medical profession and in the health services in general.

Without such protection, those in need of medical assistance may be deterred from revealing such information of a personal and intimate nature as may be necessary in order to receive appropriate treatment and, even, from seeking such assistance, thereby endangering their own health and, in the case of transmissible diseases, that of the community.

The domestic law must therefore afford appropriate safeguards to prevent any such communication or disclosure of personal health data as may be inconsistent with the guarantees in Article 8': *Z* v *Finland* (1998) 25 EHRR 371.

However, the duty to keep a patient's information confidential is not absolute. It can be overriden by public interest considerations. For example, in *Z* v *Finland* (above) the applicant was the wife of a criminal accused of sexual assaults. She resisted attempts by the police to discover her HIV status. The police seized her medical records from hospital. These were included on the court file. The court file was scheduled to be released to the public in 2002. Although art 8 of the Convention had been breached, such breach was lawful being 'in accordance with the law' within the meaning of art 8(2). The breach of the applicant's Convention rights pursued the legitimate aim of investigating and prosecuting a crime and was proportionate.

As a general rule, the public authority must not refuse to give confidential information to the individual concerned (see above).

The erosion of immunity from suits for local authorities

Blanket immunities from suit may breach the Convention (see pages 80–81). A medical practitioner may not necessarily be able to rely on his immunity, for instance, as an expert witness. In *Hughes* v *Lloyds Bank plc (Administrators of the Estate of Mukherjee)* (1998) (unreported), before the Court of Appeal, a doctor claimed immunity from a negligence suit arising out of the medical records completed by him. The plaintiff obtained the records as a preliminary to the doctor giving evidence in the plaintiff's personal injury action, which had subsequently been settled. In fact, the immunity did not bite because the plaintiff's action had been settled before proceedings were issued. In the light of *Osman* v *UK* [1998] TLR 681 arguably any such immunity claimed by a medical expert might be challenged successfully under art 6(1).

Locus standi

It might be thought that claims against doctors and hospitals would be limited, because those with the standing to bring a claim, that is the 'victims' of any breach of a Convention right, may be dead. This is not correct. As with the current domestic law, the family of the deceased may bring an action as the inheritor of the deceased's cause of action. An act which causes death and is in breach of a Convention right is likely to be a 'wrongful act, neglect or fault' within the meaning of s1 of the Fatal Accidents Act 1976. It follows that a dependency claim could be brought by the family of the deceased for breach of the Convention, even without proof of negligence or breach of duty being established. Section 8(1) HRA provides that a court may 'grant such relief or remedy, or make such order, within its powers as it considers just and appropriate'.

In the alternative, the deceased's family may be a 'victim' of the breach of the Convention in their own right and would therefore be able to bring an action against the authority (see Chapter 13).

Mental patients

Mental patients warrant special consideration. Of course they too are entitled to respect for their Convention rights, notwithstanding the lawfulness of their detention under art 5 of the Convention.

The legality of detention

Article 5(1) of the Convention permits the detention of mental patients being 'persons of unsound mind'. The ECHR take a pragmatic approach to the concept of detention:

'In order to determine whether circumstances involved a deprivation of liberty, the starting point must be the concrete situation of the individual concerned and account must be taken of a whole range of criteria such as the type, duration, effect and manner of implementation of the measure in question. The distinction between deprivation of and restriction upon liberty is merely one of degree or intensity, and not one of nature or substance': *Ashingdane* v *UK* (1985) 7 EHRR 529 at 541.

The detention of a mental patient must be 'lawful', both in the light of the domestic law, and the Convention. In *Winterwerp* v *The Netherlands* (1979) 2 EHRR 387 the ECHR considered detention lawful if: first, the patient is reliably shown by objective medical expertise to be of unsound mind; second, the patient's disorder is of a nature and degree to justify detention; and, third, the detention lasts only as long as the mental disorder persists.

The common law doctrine of necessity allows individuals to be detained as mental patients, either if they can and do consent to detention ('voluntary patients') or, alternatively, if they cannot consent to detention but do not manifestly object to treatment ('informal patients'): *Bournewood*

Community Mental Health Trust, ex parte L [1998] 3 WLR 106 and *Re F (Mental Patient) (Sterilisation)* [1990] 2 AC 1.

A detention of a mental patients under the Mental Health Act 1983 must be scrutinised for compliance with the Convention. The mere fact that the detention is pursuant to statute does not necessarily mean it is 'according to law' and lawful under the Convention.

Procedural safeguards for mental patients

Challenge to the detention

A detained mental patient has a right under art 5(4) of the Convention to 'take proceedings by which the lawfulness of his detention shall be decided speedily by the Court and his release ordered if his detention is not lawful'. The ECHR affirmed in *Winterwerp v The Netherlands* (1979) 2 EHRR 387 that:

> 'Mental illness may entail restricting or modifying the manner of exercise of the right [to access of the court and to make representations] but it cannot justify impairing the very essence of the right. Indeed, special procedural safeguards may prove called for in order to protect the interests of persons who, on account of their mental disabilities are not fully capable of acting for themselves.'

In the event of an emergency detention, a prior medical examination is not necessary: *X v UK* (1981) 4 EHRR 188. However, any detention following a period when a medical examination could have occurred will be unlawful.

The current position whereby individuals may be detained as mental patients under the common law, but have no procedural safeguards in respect of the circumstances or duration of their detention, obviously violates the Convention.

Challenge to continued detention

Burden of proof

Currently, in order to obtain his release, a detained mental patient must show that he is no longer suffering from a mental disorder. The Convention provides that an individual should not be deprived of his liberty, unless justified by falling within the exception of being of 'unsound mind'. Arguably the current burden of proof should be reversed: at present, the patient has to show that he is no longer suffering from a mental illness, but arguably the public authority should have to justify a continued detention.

Challenging the detention and its duration

The indefinite detention of a patient who is no longer suffering from a mental illness is unlawful. In *Johnson v UK* [1997] TLR 623 a schizophrenic with a psychopathic personality was lawfully detained under the Mental Health Act 1983 after his fifth conviction for an unprovoked attack on a member of the public. On review, he was found to be no longer suffering from a mental illness, but was further detained pending the availability of hostel accommodation. Article 5(1) of the Convention is not breached by deferring the release of a mental patient until hostel accommodation is found. However, as the Mental Health Tribunal could not provide accommodation and, as the patient could not challenge his detention (except at annual reviews), in practice his detention was indefinite and therefore breached art 5(1).

A mental patient is entitled to challenge his detention with reasonable expedition. Where access to court to review the lawfulness of a detention was delayed for four months, the ECHR held that there was a breach of the convention: *Koendjbihare v The Netherlands* (1990) 12 EHRR 820.

Legal representation for mental patients

In *Megyeri v Germany* (1993) 15 EHRR 584 it was suggested that the state has a positive obligation to ensure representation for mental patients. A legal representative must be able to enquire into the 'best interests' justifying a patient's treatment, possibly with the benefit of legal aid or other state funding.

Non-consensual surgery on mental patients

In *Re F (Mental Patient) (Sterilisation)* [1990] 2 AC 1 the House of Lords confirmed, that if a patient lacked the capacity to consent, medical treatment in his best interests could be lawfully given pursuant to the doctrine of necessity. Such surgery without the actual consent of the patient in itself is unlikely to breach the Convention provided that the patient has had the benefit of sufficient procedural safeguards. If a doctor treats a mental patient who does not consent (such as an informal patient), in the absence of a system of procedural checks and balances on his actions, the Convention is likely to have been violated. The current position where informal patients may be given treatment without their consent is recognised as inadequate. Lord Steyn commented that 'neither habeas corpus nor judicial review are sufficient safeguards against misjudgments and professional lapses in the cases of compliant incapacitated patients'. He suggested that the statutory protection afforded by the Mental Health Act 1983 be extended to all mental patients. In fact, in order to give treatment lawfully, a mental patient must be afforded the protection of the Convention.

In short, if a patient has capacity to consent, his refusal to accept treatment should be respected. If a patient does not have capacity to consent, a medical practitioner may administer treatment which is considered to be in the patient's best interest provided that adequate procedural safeguards are in place.

Nature of the treatment in detention

The treatment of a patient in detention must not be inhuman or degrading: *St George's Healthcare NHS Trust* v *S (No 2)* [1998] TLR 299.

In *Herczegfavly* v *Austria* (1992) 15 EHRR 437 the ECHR said:

'... the position of inferiority and powerlessness which is typical of patients confined in psychiatric hospitals calls for increased vigilance in reviewing whether the Convention has been complied with. While it is for the medical authorities to decide, on the basis of the recognised rules of medical science, on the therapeutic methods to be used, if necessary by force, to preserve the physical and mental health of patients who are entirely incapable of deciding for themselves and for whom they are therefore responsible, such patients nevertheless remain under the protection of art 3, the requirements of which permit of no derogation.'

Treatment will be lawful if a body of responsible medical opinion sanctions it. In practice, this will often be an easy test to satisfy. For example, Mr Herczegfavly was physically weak from a hunger strike and pneumonia. Nevertheless, as well as being artificially fed, he was isolated, treated without his consent and permanently strapped to a bed, without apparently being subjected to inhuman or degrading treatment!

Confidentiality and mental patients

A mental patient is entitled to respect for his private life pursuant to art 8 of the Convention and to ban confidential information being made public. If there is a conflict between a mental patient and the family member designated as the 'nearest relative', confidential information must not be given to the relative. To do so is an actionable breach of the Convention: *JT* v *UK* No 2694/95 (unreported).

Mental patients and a family life

Potentially, mental patients deprived of the facilities necessary to have conjugal rights may bring an application under art 12 of the Convention (which protects the right to found a family) in order to obtain such facilities.

Responsibility of the state for mental patients

The public authority is responsible for patients in their care and may be liable to pay damages if they come to some harm. In *X and Y* v *The Netherlands* (1985) 8 EHRR 235 a mentally handicapped applicant was unable to lodge a complaint of sexual abuse while detained in a mental institution because of a procedural rule. The ECHR held that The Netherlands was responsible for the deficiency in the legislation and had to compensate the applicant, notwithstanding that the sexual abuse was perpetrated by a third party.

Proceedings

Medical tribunals

Tribunals which determine a medical practitioner's right to practise medicine, including the General Medical Council, must observe the procedural safeguards of art 6(1) of the Convention: *Le Compte* v *Belgium* (1982) 4 EHRR 1. In particular, there must be legal representation, a public hearing and judgment, and an independent tribunal. The appearance of bias, even without actual bias, must be avoided. A defect in the initial disciplinary hearing may be corrected by an adequate appelate hearing: *Wickramsinghe* v *UK* [1998] EHRLR 338.

Disciplinary proceedings must not be unduly delayed. In *Konig* v *Germany* (1978) 2 EHRR 170 there was a ten-year delay. Article 6 of the Convention was breached. The anxiety and inconvenience caused to the applicant was compensated by a damage award of DM 30,000.

Inquests

Article 2 of the Convention requires that all suspicious deaths be investigated adequately. The current restriction of the inquest procedure to determine the manner of death (rather than establishing who was to blame for the death) may not satisfy such requirement: *McCann, Farrell and Savage* v *UK* (1995) 21 EHRR 97. It is possible that the family of the deceased or others may be able to widen the scope of the enquiry at coroner's inquests by relying on art 2.

4   Family Law

The impact of the HRA

Most recent family legislation has been drafted with the Convention in mind, and so will generally be in compliance with it. For example, the Children Act 1989 improves on earlier legislation by affording better court access to interested parties, while the Family Law Act 1996 extends protection from domestic violence to a wide range of family members.

Nevertheless, the HRA is likely to have a significant impact on the practice of family law, especially in cases involving children. Although the Convention contains no specific rights for children (by contrast with international agreements such as the UN Convention on the Rights of the Child), the right to respect for private and family life in art 8 has a key role to play in decisions to take a child into care and also in regulating contact with a child in care. These rights may also impact on contact disputes in private law proceedings. The family law practitioner will also need to take note of the operation of arts 6, 12 and 14.

Respect for family life – art 8

'Family life'

To rely on art 8 it is necessary to establish the existence of 'family life', within the meaning of the Convention. The notion of family is no longer confined to marriage-based relationships but encompasses other de facto 'family' ties, for example where the parties live together outside marriage: see *Johnston and Others* v *Ireland* (1986) 9 EHRR 203.

Beyond that, whether a relationship amounting to family life exists will depend on fact and degree. Casual relationships are less likely to qualify than stable relationships. Two cases in particular illustrate the application of these principles and how widely the concept may be drawn:

In *Keegan* v *Ireland* (1994) 18 EHRR 342 the baby of an unmarried father with no parental rights had been placed by the mother for adoption without the father's knowledge. The father wanted custody of the child but had no standing under national law to resist adoption. He alleged that his right to family life had not been respected. On the question of whether he enjoyed family life with the child, the ECHR recalled that family life could encompass arrangements where parties lived together outside marriage and continued:

> '... a child born out of such a relationship is ipso jure part of a family unit from the moment of its birth and by the very fact of it. There thus exists between the child and his parents a bond amounting to family life even if at the time of his or her birth the parents are no longer cohabiting or if their relationship has then ended.'

In that case, the important facts were that the relationship between the applicant and the child's mother had lasted for two years during one of which they lived together. Moreover, the conception of their child was the result of a deliberate decision and they had also planned to get married.

In *X, Y and Z v UK* (1997) 24 EHRR 143 family life was also found to exist between: a woman (Y) who had had a child by artificial insemination; her female to male transsexual partner (X); and the child (Z). Applying the above principles, the ECHR reasoned that X was a transsexual who had undergone gender reassignment surgery. He had lived with Y, to all appearances as her male partner, since 1979. The couple had applied jointly for, and were granted, treatment by AID to allow Y to have a child. X was involved throughout the process and acted as Z's father in every respect since the birth. In those circumstances, the ECHR held that de facto family ties linked the three applicants.

A family cannot however be based on two unrelated persons of the same sex: *S v UK* (1986) 47 DR 274 and *X and Y v UK* (1986) 32 DR 220. However, interference with such relationships will probably be a matter affecting their private lives. Article 12 is restricted in a similar way, in that the right to marry which it embodies is not applicable to homosexual unions: *Rees v UK* [1987] 2 FLR 111.

The ECHR has found family life to exist between relations such as grandparents and grandchildren, uncle and nephew etc, provided there is sufficient evidence of contact with the child and involvement in his or her life: see *Boyle v UK* (1995) 19 EHRR 179. *Eriksson v Sweden* (1989) 12 EHRR 183 has raised the possibility of an interference with the family life of a child in care and her foster parents. It will be interesting to see whether this will be raised by Mr and Mrs Bramley, the couple who have brought a claim to adopt foster children in their care who Cambridgeshire Social Services want returned.

The scope of the right

Where family life is found to exist, any interference will be unlawful unless justified under art 8(2).

The decision to take into care

The granting of a care order removing a child from its parents in order to be brought up by strangers is probably the most stark form of interference with family life possible. Accordingly, these decisions are frequently challenged for compatibility with art 8.

Where such a challenge is mounted, respondents in the UK (as opposed to Sweden, for example) have had little difficulty showing that the decision was taken in accordance with the law (ie pursuant to the Children Act 1989), or that it pursued a legitimate aim (eg to protect the child). Cases against the UK thus focus on whether the interference is 'necessary in a democratic society', ie is the interference proportionate to the aim pursued?

The ECHR has traditionally given states a wide margin of appreciation on the basis that there is no common European consensus as to the appropriateness of state intervention, and because the national courts have had direct contact with the parties concerned. Accordingly, the ECHR rarely impugns a decision to take a child into care where there has been a thorough assessment of the issue supported by expert evidence. However, the jurisprudence does establish certain principles, such as that a decision to remove a child cannot be taken simply on the basis that it would be better for the child.

Supervision following a care order

As the following cases illustrate, the ECHR consistently asserts that when a child is taken into care, the public authorities have a continuing obligation to consider the importance of resuming family life if possible. It violates art 8 to place children and then manage contact with members of their family in such a way as to make a restoration of family relationships unlikely

In *Olsson* v *Sweden* (1989) 11 EHRR 259 three children of parents with low intelligence were taken into care when each child's development was found to be significantly retarded. The ECHR did not criticise the decision to take the children into care, or the refusal to terminate care, but found a violation of art 8 in view of the measures taken to implement the care decision: namely the placement of each child separately and at a long distance from each other and their parents, and on the restrictions on the conditions of visits. As there was no question of the children being adopted, the ECHR found that the care decision should have been regarded as a temporary measure, and any measures of implementation should have been consistent with the ultimate aim of reuniting the Olsson family. The fact that the Swedish authorities had acted in good faith did not influence the ECHR's decision, and neither did the government's argument that administrative difficulties prompted the impugned decisions. On this latter point the ECHR commented that 'in so fundamental an area as respect for family life, such considerations cannot be allowed to play more than a secondary role'. (See also *Eriksson* v *Sweden*.)

In *Johansen* v *Norway* (1996) 23 EHRR 33 the applicant's mental problems led to her daughter being placed in care shortly after her birth. Three years later the applicant's situation had improved such that she was able to care for her daughter. However, in view of the time which the girl had been in care, and the little contact she had had with her mother, the domestic courts allowed the care order to stand.

The ECHR noted the wide margin of appreciation afforded to the authorities in the imposition of a care order, but stated that 'a stricter scrutiny' was called for any further limitations, such as restrictions on parental rights and access. Accordingly, the ECHR found no violation in relation to taking the child into care but considered the decision to terminate contact was unjustifiable. The risk advanced by the authorities that the applicant might disrupt the child's foster placement (which was made with a view to adoption), was not considered by the Court to be 'of such a nature and degree as to dispense the authorities altogether from their normal obligation under art 8 to take measures with a view to reuniting them if the mother were to become able to provide the daughter with a satisfactory upbringing'.

These cases suggest that that the ECHR is willing to sanction greater control of local authorities' functions once a child is in care than the domestic courts currently exercise under the Children Act 1989. It is quite possible that art 8 will encourage the domestic courts to insist that care plans should be reviewed after final care orders.

The paramountcy principle

In reaching its decision in *Johansen* v *Norway* (above), the ECHR appeared not to follow the Norwegian government's exhortation to attach paramount importance to the best interests of the child. Instead it stated that:

> '... a fair balance has to be struck between the interests of the child in remaining in public care and those of the parent in being reunited with the child. In carrying out this balancing exercise, the court will attach particular importance to the best interests of the child, which, depending on their nature and seriousness, may override those of the parent.'

An important feature of the ECHR's jurisprudence is the emphasis placed on parental rights expressed as 'a parent's right to an enduring relationship with its child'. In contrast to the traditional view of the domestic courts, the ECHR establishes that a parent as well as a child has a clear right to contact: *Peter Whitear v UK* [1977] EHRLR Issue 3; *B v UK* (1988) 10 EHRR 87; and *W v UK* (1987) 10 EHRR 29. As the following case on contact illustrates, the ECHR adopts an approach to contact disputes that differs from our own in a very fundamental way:

> 'The right to respect for family life within the meaning of art 8 of the Convention includes the right of a divorced parent, who is deprived of custody following the break-up of marriage, to have access to or contact with his child, and that the state may not interfere with the exercise of that right otherwise than in accordance with the conditions set out in paragraph 2 of that article ... the natural link between a parent and a child is of fundamental importance': *Hendricks v The Netherlands* (1982) 5 EHRR 233 (paras 94–5).

Under the Convention, therefore, the starting point is that there is a right which must be respected and must not be interfered with unless justified under para 2. The welfare of the child arises when considering whether the interference can be justified. This appears to sit uneasily with the paramountcy principle in s1(1) of the Children Act 1989 which places the welfare of the child at the centre the decision-making process.

This conflict has been examined by the national courts: see *Re KD (A Minor)* [1988] 2 FLR 139 and *R v Secretary of State for the Home Department, ex parte Gangadeen* [1998] 1 FLR 762. However, it can be predicted that as advocates become more familiar with the Strasbourg jurisprudence, art 8 will be relied on to challenge a range of decisions that involve separating a child from one or both of its parents.

Removal of a child from the jurisdiction

A specific issue that is likely to come under scrutiny in the light of art 8 is that of permanently removing a child from the jurisdiction. Since *MH v GP (Child Emigration)* [1995] 2 FLR 106 the guiding principle under English law in considering whether to grant leave has been the welfare of the child. On this basis, leave would only be withheld if the interests of the child and the custodial parent were clearly shown to be incompatible. This creates a virtual presumption in favour of the reasonable application of a custodial parent. It is certainly arguable that this does not does not accord sufficient respect for the family life of the parent who remains, the essence of family life being the right of continued contact between parent and child.

Procedural rights

Article 8 contains no explicit procedural requirements. However, the ECHR has made it clear on numerous occasions that a local authority's decision-making process must be fair and afford due respect to the interests protected by art 8. In *W* v *UK* (1987) 10 EHRR 29, for example, the local authority's failure to involve the applicant parents in the decision-making process relating to taking the child into care and in terminating access amounted to a violation of art 8, while the absence of an effective remedy led to a breach of art 6.

Similarly, *McMichael* v *UK* (1995) 20 EHRR 205 is an important case which challenges the use of 'confidential' documents in care cases. In that case the applicant parents were denied access to vital documents which included social reports on the child and recommendations for the future. This lack of disclosure was held by the ECHR to have undermined an important element of a fair trial which is 'the opportunity to have knowledge of and comment on the observations filed or evidence adduced by the other party'. This omission further created a basic inequality such that the applicant mother did not receive a fair hearing under art 6(1). (The father who was not married to the mother at the relevant time was held not to have standing in the care proceedings.) This lack of disclosure was also found to have led to the applicants being insufficiently involved in the decision-making process which led to violation of their art 8 rights: see also *Lobo Machado* v *Portugal* (1996) 23 EHRR 79.

Because of the special status of family life, these cases have consistently held that openness is required in dealings between state agencies and parents in child-care decision-making.

In fact, by virtue of the expanding concept of private life, this requirement of openness extends further. In *Gaskin* v *UK* (1989) 12 EHRR 36 the Court held that a person who has been in the care of a local authority has the right to obtain information about his or her treatment while in care. At the least, procedures must be in place to ensure that a person is not arbitrarily denied the right to know about one's background.

An important decision of the Commission which was settled before it reached the ECHR is *SD, DP and AT* v *UK* (1996) 20 May (unreported). The case concerned children who were taken into care in August 1991 and placed with temporary foster parents. An interim care order was granted in November 1991. However, a variety of administrative blunders ranging from loss of the file, difficulties in listing and other delays caused by the local authority meant that a final care order was not made until March

1993. The applicants' complaint that their right to family life was affected because their children spent prolonged period with temporary foster parents, causing them distress and uncertainty as to their future, was held admissible.

Once the HRA is in force, the creative use of Convention rights, such as arts 8 and 6, can be used to challenge decisions of the local authority and improve their decision-making processes. If these articles can be used to open up decision-making, restrict delays and in general make local authorities more accountable, a great deal will have been achieved.

Other current practices which may breach the right to a fair trial are:

• the conduct of interim care proceedings, where orders are made without oral or other evidence, given their importance in determining a child's future in the light of status quo arguments and the delays inherent in court proceedings;

• the refusal to allow oral evidence in abduction cases;

• coercion to mediation under the Family Law Act 1996 by withholding legal aid;

• restrictions such as s91(14) of the Children Act 1989 and restrictions on the rights of children to bring actions;

• hearing ancillary relief cases in chambers.

Delays in the conduct of proceedings may well breach art 6. The importance of avoiding delays where children's futures are concerned is well recognised by the ECHR and domestic courts. See Chapter 9 for important issues such as the compatibility of local authority immunity from liability in the exercise of its child-care functions with the Convention: *X v Bedfordshire County Council; M v Newham London Borough Council* [1995] 2 AC 633. The Commission has ruled the Bedfordshire and Newham applications alleging a breach of art 6 admissible, on the grounds that immunity unjustifiably denies a potential plaintiff the right of access to a tribunal, the 'very essence' of the protected right. Arguably there were also breaches of arts 3 (inhuman and degrading treatment), 8 and 13 (adequate remedy): see also *Osman v UK* [1998] TLR 681.

On procedural matters, it will also have to be considered whether the operation of powers of arrest, more widespread since the Family Law Act 1996, are compatible with the right to liberty and security of the person protected by art 5.

Positive obligations

As the cases have shown, art 8 requires more than non-interference by the state. Even if there is no deliberate act of interference, justified or otherwise, the state may still be required to take positive steps to protect and support private and family life:

> '... the object of art 8 is essentially that of protecting the individual against arbitrary interference ... nevertheless, ... respect for family life implies an obligation for the state to act in a manner calculated to allow these ties to develop normally ...': *Marckx* v *Belgium* (1979) 2 EHRR 330.

It has been seen that there is an obligation on the courts to take measures with a view to procuring and enabling contact: see also *Keegan* v *Ireland* (1994) 18 EHRR 342 and *Gaskin* v *UK* (1989) 12 EHRR 36. But the question is how far does this positive obligation extend?

Hokkanen v *Finland* [1996] FLR 289 concerned a dispute over access between the children's father and their maternal grandparents. The grandparents repeatedly refused to comply with court orders granting the father access to the children. The ECHR held that in these circumstances, the domestic authorities' failure to enforce the father's right constituted to a breach of his right to respect for his family life. The facts of this case were fairly extreme. But it is not at all clear where a positive obligation to promote contact should end. It is very unlikely that this jurisprudence requires a court to check that an intransigent parent is allowing contact. However, the only certainty is that the limits of positive obligations are inherently uncertain.

Another example of the open-ended nature of positive duties is provided by *A* v *UK* [1998] TLR 578 which established a positive duty to protect a vulnerable child. By reason of the defence of reasonable chastisement, domestic law was found to have breached art 3 by failing to protect a child against a severe beating by his stepfather who was acquitted of assault. The question arises whether art 3 (or even art 8) could be used in a similar way to found a violation if a child who was suffering neglect or emotional abuse was not removed by a local authority who knew of the neglect/abuse. Article 3 might also be used to challenge conditions in care, particularly children's homes.

Discrimination

Article 14 may also have a role to play in residence or contact disputes. For example, in *Hoffmann* v *Austria* (1993) 17 EHRR 293 a woman who lost custody of her children to their father (for reasons based essentially on the fact that she had left the Catholic Church to become Jehovah's Witness) was able to establish that there been violation of art 14 in conjunction with art 8.

Private life and atypical families

The ECHR has repeatedly said that the Convention must be interpreted in the light of present day conditions. The evolution in its treatment of atypical families illustrates the application of this principle in practice. The cases suggest that the ECHR is on the verge of finding that discrimination by states against same sex couples violates the Convention, but it has not yet done so. As a number of recent decisions illustrate, domestic law is currently consistent with the Convention.

In *Rees* v *UK* (1987) 9 EHRR 56; [1987] 2 FLR 111 a transsexual complained that the bar to changing his (formerly her) birth certificate to reflect his change of sex caused him embarrassment and humiliation whenever it had to be produced and so was a breach of his right to respect for his private life. The ECHR held that a birth certificate was a record of historical fact only, not a document showing current civil status. The complaint against the UK was thus that it refused to establish this type of documentation, but to change the system would have had wide administrative consequences. In view of the margin of appreciation (and the lack of common ground between the contracting states in this area), there was no violation of art 8. The ECHR stated, however, that the need for appropriate legal measures should be kept under review having regard to 'scientific and societal developments'. In *Cossey* v *UK* (1991) 13 EHRR 622; [1991] FLR 492 the Court reached the same conclusion but with a majority reduced from 12:3 to 10:8.

In *B* v *France* (1993) 16 EHRR 1; [1992] FLR 249 a transsexual was not permitted to alter her birth certificate, although under French law the certificate was intended to be updated throughout its holder's life. *Rees* and *Cossey* were thus distinguished and a violation of art 8 was found.

In the recent case *X, Y and Z* v *UK* (1997) 24 EHRR 143 X and Y attempted to register their child born by AID in joint names as the mother and father. However, X (a male to female transsexual) was refused permission on the grounds that only a biological man could do so. Accordingly, the register was left blank. In view of the margin of appreciation, there was no violation.

Most recently, in *Sheffield and Horsham* v *UK* (1998) 27 EHRR 163 two more transsexuals complained about the embarrassment caused by their unamended birth certificates. The ECHR followed *Rees* and *Cossey* but commented that in spite of its previous statements about keeping the legal measures this area under review, 'it would appear that the respondent state has not taken any steps to do so'. By implication, further inaction on the part of the UK taken with further developments elsewhere could tilt the balance in favour of a violation in a future case. On this basis it may be necessary to provide for changes of sex to be noted in the register and a short certificate be made available to show the new sex, a system similar to that applicable where a child is adopted.

Ancillary relief

The HRA will have little, if any, immediate impact on the resolution of property disputes on divorce. Article 5 of Protocol 7, which provides for equality between spouses and is the only provision (apart from art 14) likely to have direct relevance, has not yet been ratified by the UK and so is not contained in the 1998 Act.

Once the Protocol is ratified and implementing legislation introduced, we may see alteration to minor aspects of the present law, such as the presumption of advancement, the husband's common law duty to maintain his wife etc. Other issues which may arise include the question whether there should be an equal division of spouses assets and whether the lack of machinery to resolve property disputes between non-spouses could be seen to be discriminatory.

5   Employment Law

Introduction

The Convention rights directly affecting employment issues are contained in art 4 (prohibition of slavery and forced labour) and art 11 (freedom of association). Nevertheless, arts 6, 8, 9, 10 and 14 are also likely to have an important impact upon domestic employment law.

Application: 'public' and 'private' employers

The HRA is targeted at the misuse of power by the state. Accordingly, it does not directly protect employees against the acts of private employers (ie a claim cannot be brought against them under s6 of the HRA).

'Pure' public authorities (eg government departments, local authorities etc) must act in conformity with the Convention whether they are exercising public law or private law functions. Employees of pure public authorities can bring s6 claims against their employers. Bodies which are public authorities by virtue only of s6(3)(b) ('because certain of their functions are functions of a public nature'), 'hybrid public authorities', must comply in their public law acts but not in their private law relationships.

Forced or compulsory labour

Article 4(1) (concerning slavery and servitude) typically arises in crime. Article 4(2) (concerning forced or compulsory labour) obviously applies to employment. Article 4(3) restricts the practical utility of art 4(2). For example, in the *Boy Soldiers* case art 4(3)(b) prevented reliance upon art 4(2) despite the youth of the applicants (15 and 16 years of age) when they volunteered for military service: *W, X, Y and Z v UK* No 3435/67 (1968) 28 CD 109.

Complaints by professionals relating to onerous professional regulations are received without sympathy. The Commission has emphasised that art 4 provides no right to carry out a profession, nor a guaranteed level of remuneration. Accordingly, a dentist's complaint about being required to provide work at fixed prices and a professional footballer's complaint about the effect of a transfer fee both failed: *Iversen v Norway* 6 YB 278 (1963) and *X v The Netherlands* (1983) 5 EHRR 598.

Attempts to argue that welfare benefit provisions, requiring job seekers to accept employment or lose the right to benefits, amount to forced or compulsory labour have been unsuccessful. The necessary element of compulsion for a breach of art 4 is difficult to prove, since the Commission does not consider that such legislation forces an applicant to work, but merely deprives him of benefits: *X* v *The Netherlands* (1976) 7 DR 161 and *Talmon* v *The Netherlands* [1997] EHRLR 448. Nevertheless, welfare legislation, such as the government's 'Welfare to Work' reforms, must be scrutinised carefully.

The rights of trade unions and their members

The law concerning industrial action is governed by statute. Current legislative proposals are intended to restore some trade union rights abolished under past Conservative governments. In this area of transition it is difficult to predict the effect of the HRA. However, as seen below, the ECHR has left the states a wide margin of appreciation in the regulation of trade union rights so its body of jurisprudence may not be of great assistance to those seeking to assert new rights for unions.

Discrimination against trade union members

Article 11(1) of the Convention protects the right to freedom of association and the right to form and join trade unions.

The pending cases of *Wilson and National Union of Journalists* (Application No 30668/96) and *Palmer, Wyeth and the National Union of Rail, Maritime and Transport Workers* (Application No 30671/96) challenge personal employment contracts requiring employees to forego trade union rights. Those refusing to sign their contracts were not given pay increases. The applicants complained to the industrial tribunal of an infringement of their right not to have action taken against them on trade union grounds under s23(1) of the Employment Protection (Consolidation) Act 1978. The House of Lords decided in favour of the employers on the basis that an 'omission' to offer pay increases did not constitute an 'act' for the purposes of s23(1) of the 1978 Act. Lord Browne-Wilkinson lamented the undesirable lacuna in the legislation protecting employees against victimisation (see [1995] 2 All ER 100 at 112).

The International Labour Organisation (ILO) Committee on Freedom of Association has stated that *Wilson* reinforces its view that the UK's legislative protection against 'acts of anti-union discrimination' is 'insufficient'. The effect of the *Wilson* decision is likely to be reversed by legislation: Employment Relations Bill, introduced 27 January 1999.

The 'right to be heard'

The ECHR has adopted a narrow interpretation of art 11. The only indispensable right to have been recognised to date is the right to be heard. In the *National Union of Belgian Police* v *Belgium* (1975) 1 EHRR 578, para 39, the ECHR referred to the text of art 11 'for the protection of his interests' and stated:

> ' ... these words, clearly denoting purpose, show that the Convention safeguards freedom to protect the occupational interests of trade union members by trade union action, the conduct and development of which the contracting states must both permit and make possible ... it follows that the members of a trade union have a right, in order to protect their interests, that the trade union should be heard. Article 11(1) certainly leaves each state a free choice of the means to be used towards this end ...'

While recognising the right to be heard, the ECHR thus affords states a 'free choice of the means' to safeguard the right. In reality this has restricted the application of the so-called right to be heard. For example, in the *Belgian Police* case when the state refused to recognise the union, the ECHR held that art 11(1) did not guarantee right of union consultation. Similarly, in the *Swedish Engine Drivers' Union* v *Sweden* (1976) 1 EHRR 617, where the state concluded agreements only with the state employees' union and not with the applicant union, the ECHR held that art 11(1) does not guarantee a right to collective bargaining.

The right to be heard does not provide an unfettered right to strike, notwithstanding that the ECHR recognises the right to strike as one of the most important means of safeguarding the freedom of trade unionists to protect their interests: *Schmidt and Dahlstrom Case* (1976) 1 EHRR 578, paras 33 to 40. However, the means by which the right to strike is restricted may be challenged under art 11(1). In *National Association of Teachers in Further and Higher Education* v *UK* [1998] EHRLR 773 the Court of Appeal upheld an injunction restraining the applicant union from striking because of its refusal to give the names of the employees who would be taking part in the strike contrary to ss226A and 234A of the Trade Union Labour Relations (Consolidation) Act 1992. Sir Thomas Bingham MR sympathised with these unease of the judge at first instance as to the effect of the sections on industrial relations, but considered himself bound by the unambiguous words of the statute. The Commission granted a wide margin of appreciation and found no violation.

Once the Convention has been incorporated, the domestic court will construe restrictions on trade union rights with close regard to art 11(1) but free from the ECHR's limitation of the doctrine of the 'margin of appreciation'. Article 11(1) will be violated if there is no effective right to be heard. Proposed legislation on trade union recognition and the right to union representation at grievance and disciplinary hearings is likely: Employment Relations Bill.

Abuse of power by trade unions

The ECHR has emphasised the need for states to protect individuals from abuse of union power. However, it has avoided assessing the relative strengths of 'negative rights' (such as the right not to join a union) as against 'positive rights' (such as a union's right to attempt to ensure effective industrial action): *Cheall* v *UK* (1986) 8 EHRR 45 at 74; *Sibson* v *UK* (1994) 17 EHRR 193; and *Gustafson* v *Sweden* (1996) 22 EHRR 409. Domestic courts may be required to undertake a more critical analysis of the balance between such competing rights.

Domestic courts will however have to contend with the ECHR's inconsistent rulings on the definition of an 'association' within the meaning of art 11. For example, a body regulating medics (the 'Ordre des Médecins') is a professional regulatory body and thus not an association (*Le Compte* v *Belgium* (1982) 4 EHRR 1), but a body regulating taxi drivers is an 'association' rather than a regulatory body: *Sijurdur Sigurjonsson* v *Iceland* (1993) 16 EHRR 462.

The ECHR resolutely protects negative rights in respect of closed shop agreements. In *Young, James and Webster* v *UK* (1981) 4 EHRR 38 the ECHR held that the requirement that all employees belong to a union violated art 11. The present government appears to agree and a 'return to the closed shop' has been firmly rejected.

Restrictions under art 11(2)

The right to form and join a trade union is subject to possible restrictions under art 11(2). Such restrictions must be both 'prescribed by law' and 'necessary in a democratic society' to be lawful. A blanket denial of the right to form or join a trade union is unlikely to be lawful, but restrictions on the activities of a union, such as the regulation of strikes, might be easier to justify. In determining whether a restriction is 'necessary in a democratic society' arts 5 and 6 of the European Social Charter 1961 and conventions 87 and 98 of the International Labour Organisation may be helpful.

The second part of art 11(2), which permits 'lawful restrictions on the exercise of these rights by members of the armed forces, of the police or of the administration of the state', provides an even greater limitation on the basic right. For example, in *Council of Civil Service Unions* v *UK* (1988) 10 EHRR 269 civil servants at GCHQ were forbidden from belonging to a trade union. The application was held to be inadmissible because civil servants were 'members of the administration of the state'. The Commission's failure to distinguish between a restriction of the right to join a union and the total exclusion of such a right has been rightly criticised. As to the scope of the term 'members of the administration of the state': see *Vogt* v *Germany* (1995) 21 EHRR 205.

Equal treatment in employment

Article 14 prohibits discrimination in the enjoyment of Convention rights. It has no independent existence of its own. Thus, there is no specific prohibition against discrimination per se and, as there is no right to a job, neither is there a specific guarantee of equal treatment in employment. Nevertheless, art 14 in conjunction with art 8 (concerning respect for private and family life), art 9 (concerning freedom of thought, conscience and religion) and art 10 (concerning freedom of expression), provides effective protection against discrimination in the workplace. The ambit of art 14 provides far wider protection than current domestic legislation: it covers discrimination on the ground of 'colour ... language ... national or social minority, property, birth or other status'. An additional draft protocol including a 'non-exhaustive list of discrimination grounds' is anticipated by December 1999.

Incorporation of the Convention coincides with recent developments in EC discrimination law. Article 13 of the Amsterdam Treaty sanctions legislation to combat discrimination based on 'sex, racial or ethnic origin, religion or belief, disability, age or sexual orientation'. The Commission for Racial Equality has already produced a draft Directive to this end: 'Proposals for Legislative Measures to Combat Racism and to Promote Equal Right in the European Union'. In addition, the new art 141(4) (amending the existing art 119) of the Treaty of Rome permits member states to positively discriminate.

Discrimination on grounds of race, sex, disability and religion

Race, sex and disability discrimination are the subject of domestic legislation: Sex Discrimination Act 1975, Race Relations Act 1976 and Disability Discrimination Act 1995. Religious discrimination is prohibited only in Northern Ireland by the Fair Employment Act 1989.

Article 9 of the Convention provides an express right to freedom of religion and freedom to manifest religion or belief. Muslims (*Ahmad* v *UK* (1981) 4 EHRR 126), Jews (*Prais* v *EC Council* Case 130/75 [1976] 2 ECR 1589 (ECJ)) and Christians (*Stedman* v *UK* [1997] EHRLR 544) have relied on art 9, with varying degrees of success, in respect of working on days of religious significance. The cases turned on their own facts, but art 9 provides only a modest degree of protection in employment. In *Stedman*, for example, the applicant was dismissed for refusing to work on a Sunday. The Commission found that her dismissal 'was not based on her religious convictions as such, but on the fact that she refused to sign a contract which contained terms with which she disagreed'. In *Knudsen* v *Norway* (1986) 8 EHRR 45 at 63 the Commission went so far as to state that the applicant's freedom to relinquish his office (as a clergyman) was 'an ultimate guarantee of his right to freedom of thought, conscience and religion ...'.

Freedom of expression

Discrimination arising from an employee's politics may be challenged under arts 9 and 10. In *Vogt* v *Germany* (1996) 21 EHRR 205 the dismissal of a state teacher (who was a civil servant) because of her active membership of the German Communist Party violated arts 10 and 11. In *Ahmed, Perrin, Bentley and Brough* v *UK* [1997] EHRLR 670 the Commission admitted complaints that the Local Government (Political Restrictions) Regulations 1990, restricting the political activity of civil servants holding 'politically restricted posts', violated art 10. This decision has been seen as a significant departure from the wide margin usually granted to states in regulating the employment conditions of civil servants.

Article 10 may provide protection to 'whistleblowers' who leak confidential material contrary to the interests of their employers. However, the Public Interest Disclosure Act 1998 is likely to provide more effective protection in most cases.

Sexual orientation and transsexuals

There is no domestic, Community or Convention law specifically prohibiting discrimination on grounds of sexual orientation or 'gender reassignment'. Nevertheless, in *P v S and Cornwall County Council* [1996] All ER (EC) 397 a manager in a state college was dismissed when he announced his intention to have a sex change. The ECJ declared that 'the right not to be discriminated against on grounds of sex is one of the fundamental human rights' and that the Equal Treatment Directive applied to discrimination against transsexuals.

The ECJ distinguished *P v S* and limited its implications in *Grant v South-West Trains* [1998] All ER (EC) 193 in which a woman complained that the employer's refusal of travel concessions for her female partner infringed art 119 of the EC Treaty. Travel concessions were granted to heterosexual partners. The ECJ held that whilst sex discrimination could arise from gender reassignment, it did not apply to 'differences of treatment based on a person's sexual orientation' (para 42).

Interestingly, the ECJ attempted to justify its decision be reference to art 8 (see Chapters 4 and 12). As the cases of *Cossey v UK* (1991) 13 EHRR 622, *X, Y and Z v UK* (1997) 24 EHRR 143 and *Sheffield and Horsham v UK* (1998) 27 EHRR 163 demonstrate, the ECHR has been hesitant in finding a violation in respect of the treatment of transsexuals. However, domestic courts may be less circumspect. In *R v Ministry of Defence and Others, ex parte Smith and Others* [1996] IRLR 100 (CA) the Master of the Rolls recognised the possible application of art 8 to discrimination on grounds of sexual preference. Although this case was referred to the Commission, under the HRA it would be determined domestically.

In *R v Ministry of Defence, ex parte Perkins* [1998] IRLR 508 a homosexual serviceman was dismissed. Lightman J considered that there was a real prospect that the ECJ would hold that the Equal Treatment Directive afforded protection to Mr Perkins and invalidated the policy of discharging homosexuals from the armed forces. He considered himself bound by *Grant* to withdraw the reference to the ECJ, but added that such policy was likely to be challenged successfully in the future under powers conferred by the Treaty of Amsterdam and the European Court of Human Rights.

Privacy in the workplace

Article 8, together with the Data Protection Act 1998 and the Access to Medical Records Act 1988, may provide a check on state monitoring of the workforce. When state surveillance was challenged in *Klass* v *Germany* (1978) 2 EHRR 214, the ECHR considered that 'the mere existence of secret measures' might give rise to a claim even if, owing to the secrecy of the measures, the applicant 'cannot point to any concrete measures affecting him'. Similarly, in *Hilton* v *UK* (1988) 57 DR 108, the applicant applied for a job with the BBC and challenged the legitimacy of covert security checks by MI5 which delayed the BBC's communication of the success of her application. Telephone-tapping and searches by the police have also been challenged successfully: *Malone* v *UK* (1984) 7 EHRR 14 and *Niemietz* v *Germany* (1992) 16 EHRR 97 (and see Chapter 10).

Internal surveillance of staff by employers, such as the monitoring of telephone calls or e-mail and security checks or the abuse of CCTV, might also violate art 8. In *Boyle and Rice* v *UK* (1988) 10 EHRR 425, for example, the wrongful interference with a prisoner's mail violated art 8, and in *Halford* v *UK* (1997) 24 EHRR 523 the eavesdropping by Merseyside police on its own internal telephone system, including private calls made by the applicant employee, violated the applicant's right to private life in circumstances where there was no domestic law prohibiting such surveillance. Equally, the use of CCTV or the interception of e-mail may be open to challenge: *R* v *Brentwood Borough Council, ex parte Peck* [1997] TLR 676.

Prudent employers would be advised to review their procedure for medical checks on staff and the preservation of confidentiality relating to staff medical records. In *X* v *EC Commission* [1994] ECR 1–4737 the ECJ reaffirmed that art 8 'includes in particular a person's right to keep his state of health secret'. The Commission had violated the right to privacy of an HIV-positive candidate by carrying out tests without his consent. The storage and release of medical records has also been considered by the ECHR: *MS* v *Sweden* [1998] EHRLR 115 (concerning the release of medical records by a clinic to the Social Insurance Office) and *Chave, née Julien* v *France* (1991) 71 DR 141 (concerning the storage of hospital records and the need for confidentiality).

Right to a fair trial

In the determination of 'civil rights and obligations' art 6 provides a right to a fair and public hearing within a reasonable time by an independent and impartial tribunal. 'Civil rights' have traditionally been defined in terms of private law, rather than public law, although this distinction is being gradually eroded.

As a result of the distinction, public sector employees were often unable to rely on art 6, whereas private sector employees could. An example is civil servants: *Neigel v France* [1997] EHRLR 424 and *Balfour v UK* [1997] EHRLR 665. The HRA applies to the acts of public authorities (s6), but the employees of such authorities may not be able to rely on the fair trial provisions of art 6 to challenge those acts. As the private law/public law distinction is eroded it is anticipated that the protection provided by art 6 may become available to all. Certainly the ECHR has been more receptive to the claims of civil servants, at least in relations to claims for dismissal if not yet for claims relating to appointment (or the failure to be appointed).

It is not necessary for all tribunals to satisfy art 6. The 'demands of flexibility and efficiency ... may justify the prior intervention of administrative or professional bodies and, a fortiori, of judicial bodies which do not satisfy the said requirements in every respect ...'. At some stage, however, if only on appeal, an individual must come before a tribunal satisfying art 6(1): *Le Compte v Belgium* (above).

The statutory requirements concerning the jurisdiction, remedies and procedure of employment tribunals do not necessarily infringe art 6. In *Stedman v UK* [1997] EHRLR 544, for instance, the Commission held that the two-year continuous employment requirement for unfair dismissal claims did not prevent access to the court. Challenges under EC law have independently encouraged the government to reduce the qualifying period to one year.

An argument that art 6(1) provides for a right to legal representation before employment tribunals, and in consequence, a right to legal aid, is likely to fail. The employment tribunal process is designed for litigants in person and the law is not usually complex. Article 6 may permit a challenge to a tribunal's internal procedure and administration where this has caused injustice. Periods of long delay may also be challenged. For example, in *Darnell v UK* (1994) 18 EHRR 205, excessive delay in determining the applicant's claim for unfair dismissal against a health authority (lasting nine years and comprising various judicial review applications, including industrial tribunal and employment appeal tribunal hearings) was found to violate art 6.

See further Chapter 9.

6   Judicial Review

Introduction

Paradoxically, it is this area of the law in which the incorporation of the Convention will have both the greatest impact and the least impact. On the one hand, a breach of the Convention is effectively a new cause of action and many new cases will be brought in consequence. On the other hand, in certain types of cases, indirect regard has been had to the Convention for some time so that the formalisation of this process by the direct enforceability of Convention rights may not make a radical difference: *R v Secretary of State for the Home Department, ex parte Kevin McQuillan* (1994) The Independent 23 September.

Locus standi

The ambit of standing

It has been suggested that the test for standing of applicants for judicial review of an unlawful act violating the Convention is more stringent than that for the usual judicial review applicant.

Currently, an applicant for judicial review must have 'sufficient interest'. A generous interpretation is adopted. For example, in *R v Somerset County Council and ARC Southern Ltd, ex parte Dixon* [1997] COD 323, Sedley J stated that ' the courts have always been alive to the fact that a person or organisation with no particular stake in the issue or outcome may, without in any sense being a mere meddler, wish and be well placed to call the attention of the court to an apparent misuse of public power'. Applying this approach, applicants for judicial review have included representative bodies and public interest groups such as Greenpeace, the Equal Opportunities Commission, Help the Aged, Liberty and the Child Poverty Action Group.

An application for judicial review pursuant to the HRA has a different test for standing. In order to have sufficient interest in the unlawful act violating the Convention, s7(3) HRA requires that 'the applicant ... is, or would be, a victim of that act'. The definitions of 'victim' and 'public authority' are examined in Chapter 13 and are the same in judicial review applications. It is probable that even if the wide interpretation of 'victim' by the ECHR is adopted by the domestic court, it is likely busybodies and public interest groups cannot satisfy the 'victim' test and will therefore now be excluded from bringing judicial review applications for Convention violations.

The HRA was not intended to reduce existing rights to bring an application for judicial review. In practice, therefore, the absurd position of representative groups being able to make an application for judicial review on any ground, except that of breach of a Convention right, may be circumvented. The common law already protects certain fundamental rights, for example: free speech (*Derbyshire County Council v Times Newspapers Ltd* [1993] AC 534); right to life (*R v Secretary of State for the Home Department, ex parte Bugdaycay* [1987] AC 514); and the right of access to the court: *R v Secretary of State for the Home Department, ex parte Bugdaycay*. Representative groups may challenge acts by way of judicial review by invoking the common law protection for fundamental human rights. It is likely that the jurisprudence both under the Convention and pursuant to the HRA will then be let in by the back door.

However, judicial review applications are particularly suitable for interventions (see further Chapter 13).

Limitation

Section 7(5) HRA provides that the time limit for bringing a claim under the HRA is one year, except where there is already a shorter time limit. The usual three-month time limit for bringing an application for leave therefore continues to apply. The discretion to extend the time period obviously remains.

It is suggested that, where matters involving human rights' violations are concerned, the court will more readily grant an extension of time. The public interest and importance of human rights' issues will probably be considered a 'good reason for extending the period within which the application can be made' within O.53 r4(1) RSC. In *R v Secretary of State for the Home Department, ex parte Ruddock* [1987] 1 WLR 1482, which concerned phone-tapping, Taylor LJ stated:

> 'I am unimpressed by the reasons [for the delay]. But I have concluded that since the matters raised are of general importance, it would be a wrong exercise of my discretion to reject the application on grounds of delay, thereby leaving the substantive issues unresolved. I therefore extend the time to allow the applicant to proceed.'

Leave

The need for leave to apply for judicial review provides a filtering process to get rid of unmeritorious claims. It is supposed to be 'quick perusal' to determine whether the application is arguable and has some merit: *R v Inland Revenue Commissioners, ex parte National Federation of Self Employed and Small Businesses Ltd* [1982] AC 617.

However, leave applications for judicial review involving a violation of Convention rights risk becoming complex and lengthy. For instance, where a measure breaches a Convention right, but the consequent restriction is claimed to be 'necessary in a democratic society', a detailed assessment of the evidence justifying a breach of the Convention is needed. This is probably inappropriate at a leave application. In practice, it would be prudent either for a respondent to concede leave in such circumstances and to expedite the substantive hearing so that a proper assessment may be made, or alternatively deal with the issue of leave at the substantive hearing.

Substantive effect

New cause of action – breach of Convention rights

The violation of Convention rights by public authorities will be actionable. This provides a new and independent ground of challenge by judicial review. There may be challenge by judicial review as to the lawfulness of all the functions of a 'pure' public authority (see Chapter 13). In relation to a quasi-public authority (that is, an authority which undertakes some functions of a public nature) a judicial review application will lie, except in respect of acts of a private nature.

The public authority will have a defence to violating a Convention right if, as a result of primary legislation, the authority was required by primary or secondary legislation to act in a manner which is incompatible with the Convention: s6(2) HRA.

Where there has been an ostensible breach of a Convention right, but it is argued that such breach is a permitted exception (again, as an example, being 'necessary in a democratic society'), the domestic court must ensure that the interference with the Convention right is both justified and proportionate to the legitimate aim pursued. This is a departure. The courts must now embark on a balancing exercise which they have been keen to avoid in the past. The correct test is no longer whether there has been irrationality in the sense of *Wednesbury* unreasonableness, but whether the interference with a Convention right pursues a legitimate aim and is proportionate (see Chapter 2 for methodology of assessment).

Ultra vires

Similarly, the courts, which have always shied away from matters of politics, sociology and economics, will be forced to venture there.

A statute must be read so that it is compatible with the Convention which may involve, for example, importing procedural safeguards that were never intended or redefining a statutory term. A teleological approach must be adopted. It is likely that the courts, at least initially, will be uncomfortable with the task.

Furthermore, when assessing the lawfulness of acts of public authorities, the courts will again have to venture into new territory. Nice questions such as whether an interference with a Convention right is 'prescribed by law' or 'in accordance with the law' (see Chapter 2), and whether the interference is 'necessary in a democratic society' that is, implying 'the existence of a pressing social need' (*Sunday Times* v *UK* (1979) 2 EHRR 245) and is justified, not in the abstract, but rather in the circumstances of the particular case in question, will be determined by the courts.

When determining whether the action of a public authority is lawful, the concept of the margin of appreciation (see page 9 for definition) is of limited use. Once the Convention has been incorporated and will be monitored by the national courts (rather than a court at one remove) the margin of appreciation is otiose.

Irrationality

Bingham MR approved the 'accurate distillation' of irrationality in the context of human rights in *R* v *Ministry of Defence and Others, ex parte Smith and Others* [1996] QB 517:

> 'The court may not interfere with the exercise of an administrative discretion on substantive grounds save where the Court is satisfied that the decision is unreasonable in the sense that it went beyond the range of responses open to a reasonable decision-maker. But in judging whether the decision-maker has exceeded this margin of appreciation the human rights context is important. The more substantial the interference with human rights, the more the court will require by way of justification before it is satisfied that the decision is unreasonable in the sense outlined above.'

As this case pre-dated the HRA it may be safest for the advocate to rely on the text of the Convention directly when putting forward the permissible level of intervention (if any) with a Convention right. Clearly, the traditional domestic concept of *Wednesbury* unreasonableness has no relevance in this context.

Obviously, the usual burden of proof, where the applicant has to establish unreasonableness is reversed in the sense that the decision-maker will have to justify the nature, extent and lawfulness of an act which infringes a Convention right.

Procedural unfairness

Given the obligation to interpret legislation so that it is compatible with the Convention, it is likely that procedural safeguards will often be imported into legislation. Article 6(1) only applies to civil rights and obligations. While it is tempting to think that it has no direct use in determining issues of public law, the phrase 'civil rights and obligations' has an autonomous Convention meaning which is unaffected by the national categorisations of private or public law. The application of art 6(1) depends on the character of the right and therefore may apply in judicial review proceedings.

In any event, whether art 6(1) applies directly or not, the standards set out in art 6(1) of the Convention (see page 14 above) are likely to be interpreted as those standards of fairness that are required even under the common law. Article 6(1) is likely to be introduced into judicial review, if only by the back door.

Margin of appreciation v Wednesbury unreasonableness

It has sometimes been suggested that these two concepts are related. *Wednesbury* unreasonableness is a high standard of unreasonableness in decision-making: it is such unreasonableness that no decision-maker, having addressed his mind properly to the matter, could reasonably have made. The margin of appreciation is that discretion left in the domestic states in the enforcement of the rights guaranteed by the Convention. Conceptually they are distinct. However, they are both tools used to inhibit courts from striking down a particular decision. It is a trait of human nature to gravitate to the familiar and there is a serious risk that domestic judges will try to assimilate the margin of appreciation into the concept of *Wednesbury* unreasonableness. This would be a mistake which would lead the courts to abrogate their responsibility under the HRA. These are *distinct* concepts. There is no advantage in combining them. The rationale for the margin of appreciation disappears when the Convention is enforced by the national courts. This is an interesting academic point which need not trouble the court in practice for very long.

Proportionality

There is a recognised duty on a decision-maker to balance, on the one hand, the adverse effects of his decision on the rights, liberties or interests of individuals and, on the other hand, the legitimate purpose pursued.

Some believe that the domestic law already recognises the doctrine of proportionality. For example, in *Attorney-General* v *Guardian Newspapers Ltd (No 2)* [1990] 1 AC 109, Lord Goff stated (at 283):

> 'It is established in the jurisprudence of the European Court of Human Rights that ... interference with freedom of expression should be no more than is proportionate to the legitimate aim pursued. I have no reason to believe that English law, as applied in the courts, leads to any different conclusion.'

It is accepted that at least in certain circumstances the national court recognises the doctrine of proportionality. In *R* v *Secretary of State for the Home Department, ex parte Chahal* [1995] 1 WLR 526 a deportation which was conducive to the public good had to be balanced against the 'well founded risk of prosecution'. Similarly, in *R* v *Secretary of State for the Home Department, ex parte Leech (No 2)* [1994] QB 198 the right of access to court was not outweighed by a 'self-evident and pressing need' to interfere with prisoner's mail. Steyn LJ reviewed the jurisprudence of the ECHR (although not directly binding) and confirmed that it 'reinforces a conclusion that we have arrived at in the light of our domestic jurisprudence'.

However, proportionality as recognised in the domestic law is limited in ambit. It is categorised merely as a part of *Wednesbury* unreasonableness: *R* v *Secretary of State for the Home Department, ex parte Brind* [1991] 2 AC 696. This is to underestimate its importance. A determination of *Wednesbury* unreasonableness is completely alien to the balancing exercise to be undertaken by the courts between the competing interests. It is not helpful to muddy the waters by linking proportionality to *Wednesbury* unreasonableness within the context of the HRA.

As a rule of thumb, a public authority will act proportionately if either there is a balance between the end to be achieved and the means of achieving it, or where a particular objective can be achieved by more than one available means, and the public authority adopts the least harmful of these means.

The approach of the ECHR is illustrated by the *Sunday Times* case (above) concerning the 'necessity' of injuncting the proposed publication of information about pending thalidomide litigation. It determined that the restraint against the applicant's freedom of expression 'proves not to be proportionate to the legitimate aim pursued: it was not necessary in a democratic society for maintaining the authority of the judiciary'. It was not a question of deciding whether the injunction was unreasonable in a *Wednesbury* sense.

Similarly, in *Lithgow* v *UK* (1986) 8 EHRR 329, which concerned compensation for nationalising the shipbuilding industry, the ECHR stated: 'Clearly, compensation terms are material to the assessment whether a fair balance has been struck between various interests at stake and, notably, whether or not a disproportionate burden has been imposed on the person who has been deprived of his possessions.' Again, the function of the ECHR was purely a balancing of the interests set out in the Convention. While the domestic law requires a finding of a defect in the decision-making process (for example, perversity by the decision-maker) the ECHR is concerned only with the effect of the decision in interfering with Convention rights and whether such interference can be justified.

Common law protection of fundamental human rights

In the past judges have been obliged to use the common law to protect fundamental freedoms. For example, in *Derbyshire County Council* v *Times Newspapers Ltd* (above) the right to free speech was protected under the common law when Lord Keith asserted 'it is of the highest public importance that democratically elected body should be open to uninhibited criticism. The threat of civil action for defamation must inevitably have an inhibiting effect on free speech.' While it is understandable that, even after the HRA, judges may gravitate towards the familiar common law, care must be taken to ensure that in embracing the common law enthusiastically the principles of the Convention are not circumvented. The past efforts of the courts to strain the common law to protect human rights should not now be used as a restraining net on the protection of such rights under the Convention.

The scope of judicial review

The acts of judges may be challenged on appeal pursuant to s7(1)(a) HRA but not by way of judicial review (s9(2) HRA) except in Scotland.

Interestingly, in certain circumstances the scope (or rather lack of scope) of judicial review applications may itself breach art 6(1) of the Convention. Judicial review is restricted to assessing the quality of the decision rather than its merits. Usually it is concerned with matters of law and ill-suited to disputes of fact. However, where there is no factual dispute, judicial review proceedings will comply with art 6(1) as in *Bryan* v *UK* (1995) 21 EHRR 342.

Where there is a need for an assessment of the merits, a judicial review application will be insufficient to comply with the requirements of access to the court under art 6(1). In *W* v *UK* (1987) 10 EHRR 29 the ECHR noted that 'on an application for judicial review, the courts will not review the merits of the decision but will confine themselves to ensuring, in brief, that the authority did not act illegally, unreasonably or unfairly'. It considered that art 6(1) would be breached unless the local authority's decision could be reviewed 'by a tribunal having jurisdiction to examine the merits of the matter. It does not appear ... that the powers of the English courts were of sufficient scope to satisfy fully this requirement.'

Interlocutory relief

Interlocutory relief is available in judicial review proceedings, even at the ex parte leave stage. However, the availability of this is restricted by s12 HRA if it relates to freedom of expression. It provides that if the respondent

'is neither present nor represented, no relief shall be granted unless the court is satisfied –

(a) that the applicant has taken all practicable steps to notify the respondent, or

(b) that there are compelling reasons why the respondent should not be notified.'

Furthermore, s12(3) HRA provides that an interlocutory injunction to restrain publication should not be granted unless the court is satisfied that the applicant is likely to establish at trial that publication should not be allowed.

It is likely therefore that any application for interlocutory injunctive relief at the leave stage will be referred for an inter partes hearing. (See also Chapter 10 on privacy.)

Declarations

Although declarations have been an unfashionable remedy in recent years, they are primed for a comeback. The impact of the Convention on statutes that were drafted without regard to the Convention will be enormous and confusion over statutory obligations and prohibitions is likely. The court must read and give effect to all legislation so that it is compatible with the Convention, if it is at all possible to do so. A declaration is the most obvious method of providing statutory clarity. It follows that it is likely that the use of declarations will be more frequent.

Injunctions

Public authorities have a positive duty to act in accordance with the Convention. An injunction could be obtained by way of judicial review to compel public authorities to act in a particular way. Prior to the HRA even if an unlawful measure was quashed, the court often considered that it was not the function of the court to dictate that a public authority should behave in a particular way.

Damages

It is possible to obtain damages in judicial review proceedings, if the court considers it 'just and appropriate' (s8 HRA). However, reference should be made to the jurisprudence of the ECHR and art 41 of the Convention (see Chapter 14).

7   Environmental Law

Introduction

The Convention contains no express right to a clean environment, in contrast to, for example, s24 of the South African Final Constitution, the Stockholm Declaration 1972 and the African Charter of Human and People's Rights. However, largely through the use of art 8, a body of nascent environmental rights has emerged from the jurisprudence of the ECHR. As the cases will show, the rights revolve around the positive obligation on a state to respect a person's home and physical integrity. Their effect is to strengthen the domestic nuisance action and overcome obstacles which the litigant faces in such common law actions. Relying on arts 6 and 10, the ECHR has also created a body of cases which grant important procedural rights, such as participation in decision-making about environmental matters, and rights to the provision of information about risks that pollution can pose.

Article 8 and the substantive right

The first case in which the ECHR adjudicated an environmental nuisance claim was in 1990 in *Powell and Rayner* v *UK* (1990) 12 EHRR 355. Both applicants lived near Heathrow airport: Powell in Esher in a low-noise annoyance area, Rayner on a farm in Berkshire in an area of high-noise annoyance. The ECHR found that the quality of the applicants' private lives and the scope for enjoying the amenities of their homes had been adversely affected by the noise and that art 8 therefore applied. Whether the interference was justifiable required a fair balance to be struck 'between the competing interests of the individual and of the community as a whole', while granting the state a wide margin of appreciation. In view of government measures taken to abate noise pollution and compensate residents for disturbance, and given the importance of Heathrow for the economic well-being of the entire UK, there was no breach found.

Rayner was applied in *S* v *France* (1990) 65 DR 250 where the applicant complained about the siting and operation of a nuclear power station 300 metres away from her eighteenth-century house on the banks of the Loire. The erection of 120-metre high steel and concrete cooling towers; the permanent operating noise and intermittent noises, such as tannoy announcements and sudden releases of steam; the industrial lighting which remained on at night; and the loss of direct sunlight all prompted her to complain of a violation of her right to respect for her home, under art 8, and her right under art 1 of the First Protocol to the peaceful enjoyment of her possessions.

The ECHR classed the noise and other nuisance complained of as an interference with her art 8 rights. However, bearing in mind that the applicant had been awarded some FF250,000 the interference was not disproportionate to the legitimate interest in the operation of a power station.

The development of clear environmental rights took a leap forward with the decision in *Lopez-Ostra* v *Spain* (1994) 20 EHRR 277, where the ECHR unanimously found a breach of art 8. The applicant lived in Lorca, a town with a heavy concentration of leather industries. To service this industry, a waste-treatment plant was built 12 metres from the home where she lived with her husband and two daughters. The plant was owned by a private limited company but was built on municipal land and constructed with the benefit of state subsidies. In 1988 the plant began operating without a licence and, due to a malfunction, it released fumes, vile smells and contamination which made living conditions unpleasant and caused a number of local residents, including the applicant's daughter, to become seriously ill.

The applicant alleged a violation of her right to respect for her home and her physical integrity on the grounds of the regulatory authority's failure to act.

The ECHR accepted evidence before it that hydrogen sulphide emissions from the plant exceeded the permitted limit and could endanger the health of local inhabitants, but went on to assert that 'naturally, severe environmental pollution may affect individuals' well-being and prevent them from enjoying their homes in such a way as to affect their private life adversely, without, however, seriously endangering their health': para 51.

Furthermore, the ECHR was not unduly troubled by the fact that the regulatory authority, and particularly the Lornca municipality, were not directly responsible for the emissions. In order to establish a violation, it seemed to rely on the fact that the town had permitted construction of the plant on its land and with the help of state subsidies. However, it is not clear whether the ECHR accepted the applicant's submission that by virtue of the general supervisory powers conferred on the municipality by legislation, it had a duty to act.

The ECHR was clear that it was for the domestic court to determine the lawfulness of the building and operation of the plant given its failure to obtain a licence. Even if the municipality had fulfilled the functions assigned to it, the question for the ECHR was whether the national authorities had adequately protected the applicant's right to respect for her home and for her private and family life. In the ECHR's view, they had not. Furthermore, the regulatory authority had resisted judicial decisions by appealing two separate orders to close the plant in 1991.

Despite the margin of appreciation, the state did not strike a fair balance between the town's economic well-being and the applicant's individual rights. Although the plant was built to solve serious pollution problems due to the concentration of tanneries, it had from the outset, caused a nuisance and health problems for local people.

As regards the alleged violation of art 3, the ECHR held that the conditions the applicant lived in with her family were certainly very difficult, but did not amount to degrading treatment within the meaning of art 3.

The case was followed in *Guerra v Italy* (1998) 26 EHRR 357, another important case, in which a violation of art 8 was established. The applicants lived in Manfredonia, one kilometre away from an Enichem factory producing fertilisers. In 1976 an explosion at the plant had caused 150 people to be hospitalised for acute arsenic poisoning. The applicants focused on the regulator's failings under the Italian law in implementing the 'Seveso Directive' on major accident hazards, and in particular the requirement to inform local inhabitants of the details of the hazard posed by operation of the plant, safety measures and plans for emergencies, and procedures to be followed (including evacuation of inhabitants) in the event of an accident. In the light of the regulator's failure to provide this information, the applicants alleged violations of arts 2 and 10, while the court of its own motion considered, and found, a violation of art 8.

In addition to the facts above, the ECHR noted a report of technical experts which confirmed that emissions from the factory were often channelled towards Manfredonia. Thus, the ECHR concluded 'the direct effect of toxic emissions on the applicants' right to respect for their private and family life means that art 8 is applicable.' While the authorities cannot be said to have 'interfered' with this right, they failed to take steps to ensure effective protection of the applicants' rights. The Court stated:

> 'The applicants had waited, right up until the production of fertilisers ceased in 1994, for essential information that would have enabled them to assess the risks they and their families might run if they continued to live at Manfredonia, a town particularly exposed to danger in the event of an accident at the factory.'

The majority of the Court held the other articles to be inapplicable. However, two judges, Walsh and Jambrek, delivered dissenting judgments, which were particularly interesting for their views on art 2. Jambrek called for the evolution of the ECHR's case law on art 2, observing that 'the protection of health and physical integrity is as closely associated with the "right to life" as with the respect for private and family life.'

As regards art 10, both judges concurred with the majority view that art 10 did not impose any positive obligation on states to impart information. However, Jambrek proposed a gloss that this be 'save when a person of his/her own will demands/requests information which is at the disposal of the government at the material time': see *LCB v UK* [1998] TLR 381.

Under domestic law there are numerous provisions which require public authorities to disclose information about the environment and the impact on it by industrial operations, most notably the Access to Environmental Information Regulations 1992, the integrated pollution control regime and the requirements of the Environmental Impact Assessment. Whether the refusal or failure by a public authority to disclose information in an individual case would be compatible with the Convention will be for the courts to decide.

The cases outlined above are important, particularly in view of the difficulties that plaintiffs face in raising a claim against a public authority for a failure to act upon a statutory power. At common law many such claims fail when the court refuses to find a duty of care: see, for example, *Lam v Brennan and Torbay Borough Council* [1997] PIQR 488. Indeed, in *Hunter v Canary Wharf* [1997] AC 655, Lord Cooke gave a strong indication of the future when he suggested, in vain, that art 8 supported treating residence as a sufficient interest to mount a claim in private nuisance.

Procedural rights

Both arts 6 and 8 give rise to procedural rights in the environmental context.

The most important right is access to justice. Article 6 permits a complaint that an applicant has not been given a hearing or a fair hearing of his or her 'civil rights'. To date, the cases before the ECHR from the UK have mainly concerned the compatibility of planning procedures with art 6(1).

In *Fredin v Sweden* (1991) 13 EHRR 784 the applicant was the owner of a gravel pit, the exploitation of which was restricted by the Nature

Protection Acts. Between 1980 and 1983 the applicant invested large sums of money in the business, for example to improve access to the pit. However, in 1983 the applicant was informed that exploitation had to cease by the middle of the following year and that he would be required to pay further large sums as security to finance the restoration of the site after closure. The ECHR found that the absence of procedures to judicially review the decisions to revoke the permit or require security amounted to a violation of art 6.

In the UK context, *Bryan* v *UK* (1995) 21 EHRR 342 was a very important decision. This case was directly concerned with the adequacy of proceedings to challenge an enforcement notice. The applicant, who was a farmer in Warrington, Cheshire, was required by the local planning authority to demolish two brick buildings which were alleged to have been built without planning permission and which the authority considered to look like the start of a small housing estate rather than agricultural barns described by the applicant. The applicant appealed against the enforcement notice to the Secretary of State who appointed an inspector to conduct an enquiry and determine the appeal. The applicant then appealed the inspector's decision to the High Court, but on advice did not challenge the inspector's findings of fact.

There was no question that the 'impugned planning proceedings' involved a determination of the applicant's civil rights so that art 6(1) was applicable (compare *Powell and Rayner* (above) where the exclusion of liability under the Civil Aviation Act meant there was no 'civil right' to attract the application of art 6). On the substance of the complaint, the ECHR found that the inspector did not constitute an 'independent and impartial tribunal' for the purposes of art 6(1) by reason of the Secretary of State's power to revoke his authority at any time during the proceedings. However, this 'defect' was cured by the High Court review which the ECHR found to comply with art 6(1).

However, this case does not mean that the availability of judicial review (or a statutory appeal of this nature) will always ensure that a regulator's decision-making is in compliance with art 6. It is not far fetched to imagine cases where a violation might be found, for example, where the initial fact-finding is not in the form of a quasi-judicial hearing (as in the present case) and where there is a dispute on the facts. This scenario may well be a ground to distinguish *Bryan*, which was clearly concerned with a dispute of law – the application of policy to agreed facts and for which judicial review was an ideal remedy.

The right to peaceful enjoyment of possessions

Article 1 of the First Protocol has been raised in numerous environmental cases but with little success. The right it defines is a qualified one which permits significant limitations on its exercise 'in the public interest' or 'in the general interest'. To date it has been of limited practical use in environmental litigation.

In *Powell and Rayner v UK* the applicants' claim under that provision was declared in admissible with the words '[art 1 of the First Protocol] does not, in principle, guarantee a right to the peaceful enjoyment of possessions in a pleasant environment'. However, the Commission pointed out that 'noise nuisance which is particularly severe in both intensity and frequency may seriously affect the value of real property or even render it unsaleable or unusable and thus amount to a partial expropriation.'

European Community law

In addition to possible action under the HRA, European Community law provides an array of remedies of its own which have the advantage of being both more specific and easier to enforce (see Chapter 12).

The growing body of EC directives on environmental protection provide great scope for those complaining to have been affected by pollution or who make it their business to defend the environment. For example, where regulatory authorities have acted in contravention of directly effective environmental directives (eg the Urban Waste Water Directive, Groundwater Directive etc), this can provide a ground of challenge by way of judicial review. The state is afforded no margin of appreciation, the legal obligations contained in the directives are clear and must be applied by the member state, and any failure to do so may render the state liable in damages.

Environment groups are increasingly sponsoring such litigation which can lead to expensive delays and possible revocation of permits for industrial operators. An advantage for them of a challenge based on EC law is the more favourable standing requirements than under the Convention and the HRA. The experience of a single such group, Greenpeace, illustrates this clearly. The HRA limits a claim against a public authority under s7(1) to those who are 'victims' of the unlawful act, 'victim' being defined as a person who is 'directly affected'. In *Greenpeace Schweiz v Switzerland and Others* (1997) 23 EHRR CD 116 the Human Rights Commission refused to award Greenpeace standing (the ECJ's standing requirements have also excluded Greenpeace). Contrast this with the wider test of 'sufficient interest' to bring a claim in domestic judicial review proceedings, which led Otton J to grant Greenpeace standing to challenge a decision that British Nuclear Fuels could intensify its activities at its plant in Sellafield in Cumbria: *R v HMIP, ex parte Greenpeace (No 2)* [1994] 4 All ER 329; [1994] Env LR 76.

See further Chapters 6 and 8.

8   Land Law

Introduction

Land law practitioners will be principally concerned with art 8 of the Convention and art 1 of the First Protocol. Other areas of practice may be more immediately affected by the HRA, but the ECHR has considered a number property cases from the UK, and with further property law reform in contemplation it is likely that both new and existing legislation and case law will be subject to HRA challenges.

Article 1 of the First Protocol

As seen in Chapter 2, art 1 of the First Protocol grants a qualified right to the peaceful enjoyment of one's possessions and prohibits the state from depriving a person of his possessions other than in the public interest, and/or to control the use of property in the general interest.

Peaceful enjoyment of possessions and deprivation of property

The right to peaceful enjoyment of possessions includes not only the right to have and use possessions but also the right to sell, lend, hire or destroy them. The Convention protects the right to enjoy possessions free from interference by the state. Although art 1(1) speaks of protection against the deprivation of property, art 1 has been used to challenge interference which does not amount to deprivation. In an admittedly extreme case, the ECHR recently held that the burning of property by Turkish security forces engaged in a campaign against Kurdish separatists amounted to an interference with the peaceful enjoyment of possessions: *Selcuk and Asker* v *Turkey* (1998) 26 EHRR 477. However, much less dramatic measures can also amount to an interference.

For example, in *Sporrong and Lonnroth* v *Sweden* (1982) 5 EHRR 35, the applicants' properties were subject to expropriation orders to secure redevelopment of Stockholm city centre. The expropriations were not executed but while in force the owners were prevented from beginning construction on the sites which were of course blighted. This state of limbo continued for 23–25 years in one case and eight to ten in the other. Perhaps surprisingly the ECHR did not construe the measures as a 'control on use' or 'deprivation' but found interference with peaceful enjoyment of the property. In spite of the wide margin granted to the state in town planning matters the inflexibility of the Swedish system which left the applicants in a state of uncertainty for very prolonged periods, without compensation or any legal redress, did not strike a fair balance.

It seems that the protection of art 1 only extends to the economic value of property. In *S* v *France* (1990) 65 DR 250 the Commission considered the effects on the value of a property due to noise nuisance but did not even address the issue of whether a reduction in the aesthetic quality of an area caused by an industrial development could be an interference with peaceful enjoyment of property. As seen in Chapter 7, such interference may well violate the right to respect for a person's home and their physical integrity.

Although not contained in the wording of the sections, the jurisprudence of the ECHR has regularly applied the concepts of proportionality and fair balance when assessing claims made under art 1.

The availability of compensation is generally an essential element in achieving a fair balance between individual and state. In *Lithgow* v *UK* (1986) 8 EHRR 329 the applicants complained that nationalisation of their property under the Aircraft and Shipbuilding Industries Act 1977 violated their rights under art 1 on the grounds of the grossly inadequate compensation they were granted. The ECHR held that inadequate compensation could be justified by the public interest:

'Compensation must normally be reasonably related to the value of the property taken, but protocol 1, art 1, does not guarantee full compensation in all cases. Legitimate objectives of public interest may justify reimbursement at less than the full market value; the nature of the property taken and the circumstances of the taking may be taken into account in holding the balance between public and private interests ... the Court will respect the national legislature's judgment in this respect unless manifestly without reasonable foundation.'

In *Holy Monasteries* v *Greece* (1994) 20 EHRR 1 Greece had passed legislation creating a presumption of state ownership of disputed monastic lands. The ECHR held that the failure to provide compensation did not comply with the fair balance test by placing too great a burden on the monasteries, and thus violated art 1.

In the public interest

A state may deprive its subjects of their possessions if the act is in the public interest. The ECHR is very reluctant to interfere with a national government's view of what is in the national interest. In *Lithgow* v *UK* (above) the ECHR rejected arguments that it should hold that the UK government's nationalisation of the shipbuilding industry was not in the public interest. Likewise, in *James* v *UK* (1986) 8 EHRR 123, English landowners unsuccessfully challenged the Leasehold Reform Act 1967 which was designed to transfer property rights from one individual to another in order to enfranchise holders of long leases. The ECHR held that it would respect the domestic legislature's judgment as to what was in the public interest unless the legislature's view was 'manifestly without reasonable foundation'. The ECHR held that legislation aimed at enhancing social justice could properly be regarded as in the public interest.

Legislation levying a windfall tax on profits of the privatised utilities may be challenged under art 1.

Provided for by law/international law

The state must be able to point to the legal basis in domestic law for its action in depriving someone of its property. The taking of property must not be arbitrary. However, the ECHR held in *James* v *UK* (above) that the reference to a prohibition on deprivation, unless in accordance with the general principles of international law, cannot be relied upon by a national against an act of their own state: this provision only applies to the appropriation of alien property.

Control of use

Article 1(2) gives sweeping powers to the state to control the use of property, for example through planning, rent and building controls. These powers are subject only to the requirement that laws controlling the use of property are in the general interest or are to secure the payment of taxes, contributions or penalties. Although legislation which was discriminatory in its effect could fall foul of other articles of the Convention, the wording of art 1(2) is extremely wide. Again, the ECHR has held that the doctrine of fair balance applies to a consideration of whether there has been a breach under the terms of art 1(2).

In *Fredin* v *Sweden* (1991) 13 EHRR 784, for example, the ECHR held that the revocation of the applicant's gravel exploitation permit to restrain an activity which damaged the environment did not deprive him of his possessions but rather amounted to a control of their use in the general interest – a limitation provided for expressly on art 1 of the First Protocol.

Furthermore, such control had a legitimate aim in the light of the fact that 'in today's society the protection of the environment is an increasingly important consideration' (para 48) and respected the fair balance test.

It will be interesting to see whether protection of animal welfare would be considered to justify interference with the use of private property which the proposed ban on fox-hunting is likely to entail. If this legislation in enacted, a challenge under art 1 must be inevitable.

In a number of cases the ECHR has considered housing legislation that had the effect of staggering the enforcement of possession orders against tenants so as to prevent a large number of people becoming homeless at one time. In *Mellacher* v *Austria* (1989) 12 EHRR 391 the ECHR stated:

'... the second paragraph reserves to states the right to enact such laws as they deem necessary to control the use of property in accordance with the general interest. Such laws are especially common in the field of housing, which in our modern societies is a central concern of social and economic policies. In order to implement such policies, the legislature must have a wide margin of appreciation both with regard to the existence of a problem of public concern warranting measures of control and as to the choice of the detailed rules for the implementation of such measures.'

See also *Spadea* v *Italy* (1995) 21 EHRR 482 and *Scollo* v *Italy* (1995) 22 EHRR 514.

Article 8 and protection of the home

Article 8 is principally concerned with the protection of private and family life and is dealt with in more detail in other chapters (see especially Chapters 4, 7 and 10). However, it is also of relevance to land lawyers because of the protection it gives to an individual's home. It is this provision that gives the greatest scope to land lawyers to deploy Convention arguments in the domestic courts.

Respect for the home

It has been seen that an individual is entitled to access and occupation of his home: *Wiggins* v *UK* (1978) 13 DR 40. Respect for home life also includes the peaceful enjoyment of ones home. See Chapter 7 for cases illustrating different types of nuisance found to breach art 8. See also *Buckley* v *UK* (1996) 23 EHRR 191 where a gypsy complained that the refusal of planning permission which required her to move her caravan violated her right to respect for her home, and *R* v *North and East Devon Health Authority, ex parte Coughlan* [1998] New Law Digest 14 December.

Article 8 does not, however, confer the right to a home which the applicant does not already occupy or possess.

Local authorities, as providers of public housing, are particularly likely to face actions under art 8 brought on the basis of their failure to properly respect the home life of their tenants. It has been seen that, affording respect for home life can require positive actions by a public body. A tenant affected by neighbour nuisance could, therefore, argue that a local authority's failure to bring proceedings against the offending tenant amounted to a failure to respect his or her home life. Similarly, it may be argued that the government's failure to enact legislation to deal with the problem of leylandii trees means that those affected by them are unable to enjoy their home.

If there has been an interference with an individual's right to respect for their home life the authority will, of course, have to justify the interference as being in accordance with the law and necessary in a democratic society to achieve one of the aims set out in art 8 (2).

9   Civil Procedure

Introduction

The current rules of civil procedure are subject to the Convention. The most important of these are art 6(1), which provides for a right to a fair hearing, and art 8, which protects privacy. The new Civil Procedure Rules coming into force in April 1999, as well as the current rules, must be scrutinised for compliance with the Convention.

Locus standi

A person requiring the determination of his civil rights and obligations must have a forum in which can effectively determine his claim. In *Keegan* v *Ireland* (1994) 18 EHRR 342 the father of a child offered for adoption (without the father's knowledge or consent) had no standing in the adoption procedure. He was able to bring guardianship and/or custody proceedings however 'by the time these proceedings had terminated the scales concerning the child's welfare had tilted inevitably in favour of the prospective adoptors.' The father's exclusion from the adoption proceedings was held by the ECHR to have breached art 6(1).

Qualifying periods

A minimum qualifying period before a claim can be brought does not necessarily restrict access to the court so as to breach art 6(1). In *Stedman* v *UK* [1997] EHRLR 544 the Commission held that a requirement that an applicant be employed for two years before being able to bring claims for unfair dismissal or redundancy did not breach the applicant's effective right of access to the court.

Requirement of leave

Similarly, a mere requirement that leave be obtained before proceedings are issued does not necessarily infringe art 6(1).

For example, in *Ashingdane* v *UK* (1985) 7 EHRR 529 a requirement of leave which should only be granted on 'substantial grounds' under the Mental Health Act 1959 for a mentally ill patient wishing to bring an action in negligence against the hospital caring for him was not an unlawful restriction of access to court.

Similarly, in *Lithgow* v *UK* (1986) 8 EHRR 329, where individual shareholders seeking compensation were excluded from the collective arbitration provided for by legislation, art 6(1) was not breached because the shareholders' rights were adequately protected by the compensation system actually adopted. The limitation on access to the arbitration system was justified by the legitimate aim of avoiding a multiplicity of claims by shareholders. The compensation system adopted was proportionate.

Time limits

Obviously limitation periods restrict access to the court because an individual will not be able to bring an action if he is out of time. However, time limits do not necessarily breach art 6(1). The legitimate aims of time limits are to provide certainty (so that potential defendants do not have the prospect of limitation hanging over them indefinitely), and to prevent the risk of injustice where the court is forced to make a determination on oral evidence from impaired memories or on incomplete documentation where relevant documents have been lost or destroyed.

For example, in *Stubbings* v *UK* [1998] TLR 579, the alleged victims of child sexual abuse could not bring an action because by the time the applicants suffered the psychological after-effects of abuse and realised that they had a cause of action, the action was statute-barred. The ECHR considered that the limitation rules pursued a legitimate aim of ensuring legal certainty and finality and that the limitation rules were proportionate. There was therefore no breach of art 6(1) and the limitation rules were lawful.

However, if the time limit is too short or too strict, art 6(1) may be breached. For example, in *Perez de Rada Cavanilles* v *Spain* (1998) 28 October (unreported) the 'particularly strict application' of a three-day time limit to apply to set a judgment aside breached art 6(1).

Access to a solicitor

In *Golder* v *UK* (1975) 1 EHRR 524 there was a breach of art 6(1) when a prisoner was not allowed to see a solicitor in order to start an action. Although there was no formal ban on bringing an action, in fact, there was an impediment to bringing an action, if only by means of a temporary delay. The right to legal representation requires not merely the presence of a lawyer but actual and effective legal representation: see *Artico* v *Italy* (1980) 3 EHRR 1.

Legal aid

Some people cannot afford to litigate without public funding. When such funding is not available then, depending on the circumstances of the case, art 6(1) may be breached.

In *Airey* v *Ireland* (1979) 2 EHRR 305 the ECHR found that art 6 had been violated because Mrs Airey did not have legal aid in order to get a judicial separation from her husband. The ECHR noted that the proceedings were complex, involving difficult points of law and expert witnesses requiring skilled cross-examination. Her emotional involvement with the case was also incompatible with the objectivity needed for forensic advocacy. This case does not mean that there is a universal right to legal aid. Sometimes litigants in person without the benefit of public funding will still have effective access to the court and art 6(1) will not be infringed. However, the ECHR determined 'art 6(1) may sometimes compel the state to provide the assistance of a lawyer when such assistance proves indispensible for an effective access to court ... by reason of the complexity of the procedure or of the case ...'.

In *Stewart Brady* v *UK* (1997) 24 EHRR CD 38 the plaintiff's action was struck out on the grounds that it had no reasonable prospect of succeeding and that the costs were disproportionate to the amounts involved. The plaintiff wanted to appeal and was refused legal aid. The ECHR found that there was no violation of art 6(1).

Jurisdiction

Sometimes the court does not have the jurisdiction to investigate and determine matters as fully as the litigant might wish. If the court cannot determine the facts and legal matters that are in issue, there may be a violation of the right of access to court. In *Tinnelly* v *UK* [1998] TLR 437 the applicant, who was unsuccessful in tendering for a public works contract, complained to the Fair Employment Agency that it had been subject to political and religious discrimination. The Secretary of State certified that the tender had been rejected on the grounds of national security. The FEA deemed the certificate to be conclusive of the reason for the rejection of the tender. If a judge were to consider an application for judicial review he would also deem the certificate to be conclusive. The ECHR considered that there had been a breach of art 6(1); there was no opportunity to scrutinise the factual basis of the certificate. While acknowledging the importance of the security considerations, the ECHR considered that the conclusive nature of the certificate had a disproportionate effect on the applicant's right of access to the court to have a judicial determination of the substantive merits of the claim that they had suffered unlawful discrimination. The right of access to a court could not be displaced on the say so of the executive even if national security considerations played an important part in the case.

Similarly, in *W v UK* (1987) 10 EHRR 29 the applicant, whose children were in care, was prevented from having contact with them. He could bring judicial review proceedings or wardship proceedings in which the court would assess the quality (or otherwise) of the decision by the local authority. The court could not however assess the merits behind the decision. The ECHR noted that 'on an application for judicial review, the courts will not review the merits of the decision but will confine themselves to ensuring, in brief, that the authority did not act illegally, unreasonably or unfairly ... the scope of the review effected in wardship proceedings will normally be similarly confined.' The ECHR considered that art 6(1) would be breached unless the local authority's decision could be reviewed 'by a tribunal having jurisdiction to examine the merits of the matter. It does not appear ... that the powers of the English courts were of sufficient scope to satisfy fully this requirement during the currency of the parental rights resolution.'

However, where there is no factual dispute, judicial review proceedings will comply with art 6(1), for example in many environmental and planning cases: see *Bryan v UK* (1995) 21 EHRR 342.

Immunities

Article 6(1) does not create new causes of action. The substantive definition of legal rights are unaffected. However, procedural bars to a remedy (where there is an existing legal right) may breach art 6(1). The distinction is not always an easy one to make.

In the past, local authorities have had immunity from suit in respect of their tortious acts in performing their statutory duties. In *X v Bedfordshire County Council* [1995] 2 AC 633 Lord Browne Wilkinson said '... statutory provisions establishing a regulatory system of a scheme of social welfare for the benefit of the public at large [do not] give rise to a private right of action for damages for breach of statutory duty.' Actions against local authorities have therefore failed, even where the local authority has been negligent. Such a blanket immunity may well be eroded by art 6(1).

In *Osman v UK* [1998] TLR 681 the plaintiffs complained that the negligence of the police in carrying out their duties permitted a family member from being murdered by one Paget-Lewis. Their claim against the police had been struck out because the police had an immunity from suit. The ECHR found that a blanket immunity from suit violated art 6. The national court must be able to weigh competing public interest considerations and to ensure that any immunity given is proportionate: 'it must be open to a domestic court to have regard to the presence of other public interest considerations which pull in the opposite direction to the application of the rule [providing immunity]'. The scope of the police immunity from suit (although having a legitimate aim) was disproportionate.

Not all immunities from suit will breach art 6(1). In *Fayed* v *UK* (1994) 18 EHRR 393 Mr Fayed's defamation action was defeated by the Department of Trade and Industry's immunity from suit provided by the doctrine of qualified privilege for investigators' reports. Although the ECHR held that art 6 may be breached if the courts 'remove from the jurisdiction of the courts a whole range of civil claims or confer immunities from civil liability on large groups or categories of persons', it considered the immunity conferred by qualified privilege to be a lawful restriction. The legitimate aim of encouraging the inspectors to report 'with courage and frankness' which was protected by qualified privilege was a proportionate restriction of access to the court. It appears therefore that blanket immunities from suit will violate art 6 unless they are necessary to pursue a legitimate aim and are proportionate.

In *National Provincial Building Society* v *UK* [1997] STC 1466 legislation was introduced which (as Parliament had intended from the outset) validated tax regulations which had been defective. The legislation had retrospective effect. Various claims for restitution were therefore barred. However, such action did not breach art 6(1).

Security for costs

If the person bringing a claim is poor, an order for security for costs is likely in practice to bar access to the court. However, the ECHR found that, at least in respect to appelate proceedings, art 6(1) is not violated: see *Tolstoy Miloslavsky* v *UK* (1995) 20 EHRR 442. However, it might be a violation of art 6(1) if, in practice, it bars the access to court at first instance, as in *Ait-Mouhoub* v *France* (1998) 28 October (unreported).

Dismissal for want of prosecution

Article 6(1) requires a hearing within a reasonable time. Plaintiffs sometimes proceed slowly and, in practice, the defendant has no remedy. For example, the claim of a plaintiff under a permanent disability cannot be dismissed for want of prosecution following the Court of Appeal authority of *Turner* v *W H Malcolm Ltd* (1992) 136 SJ. The Civil Procedure Rules after April 1999 will not allow such a delay. Arguably an application for dismissal for want of prosecution is a determination of the defendant's civil rights and obligations so that a defendant may rely on art 6(1) to obtain a dismissal for want of prosecution. A defendant would not have to prove inordinate and inexcusable delay, contumelious default or prejudice, merely that there has not been a hearing within a reasonable time.

Delay in the proceedings does not automatically mean that there has been an unreasonable delay contrary to art 6(1) of the Convention. In *Proszak* v *Poland* (1997) 16 December (unreported) in spite of civil proceedings taking three years, nine months and two weeks, art 6 was not breached. The delay was reasonable: first, the legal representatives had acted reasonably and had not been inactive; second, the applicant being unco-operative (for example, by refusing to be examined by another medical expert) had caused delay; and, third, the case was sufficiently complex to justify a delay for further specialist medical opinion to be obtained.

This case should be contrasted with *Darnell* v *UK* (1993) 18 EHRR 205 where, following his dismissal from a health authority, the applicant brought several judicial review applications and his claim before the industrial tribunal was appealed to the Employment Appeal Tribunal. The proceedings took a total of nine years. This was held to be an unreasonable delay in violation of art 6. The ECHR does not discount time taken by appeals. All the time taken to resolve the matter is considered.

Article 6(1) may also be useful in resisting applications for an extension of time for carrying out steps in litigation.

Hearings in chambers

Article 6 provides for judgments to be made in public. The domestic court practice probably complies with this obligation, even in respect of interlocutory applications heard in chambers. In *Hodgson and Others* v *Imperial Tobacco* [1998] 1 WLR 1056 it was held that hearings in chambers were hearings to which the public were not routinely admitted as of right as a matter of administrative convenience, but the substance of the hearings was not confidential (save in exceptional circumstances) and could and should be disseminated to the public.

In practice, many hearings are heard without the public being admitted. As long as the public can be admitted to the hearing it is thought that art 6(1) is not breached. It does not matter whether the public are in fact there or not.

Evidence and disclosure

Protection of the privacy of the individual

Individuals are entitled to protection of privacy pursuant to art 8 of the Convention. This may mean that the current rules of discovery (which extend to anything that would prompt a line of enquiry) will be too wide. In particular, the discovery of medical records may be limited. In *MS* v *Sweden* (1997) 3 BHRC 248 the applicant's medical history and medical records were held to be part of her private life. Surprisingly, the applicant was held not to have waived her right to insist on the non-disclosure of the medical records notwithstanding that she had brought a personal injury action. It is likely that art 8 of the Convention limits discovery of medical records to only those relevant to the actionable injury. At present, all medical records are discoverable. It is noted that the Civil Procedure Rules limit the ambit of discoverable documents in standard disclosure to, in effect, those that support the plaintiff and those that might support the defendant. The spirit of discovery after April 1999 is for relevant, rather than wholesale, discovery.

The access by an individual to documents

In spite of the domestic law, it is sometimes difficult for an individual to obtain information and records about himself. An applicant may rely on arts 6 and 8 of the Convention in order to get wider disclosure than he would otherwise obtain: see *McGinley* v *United Kingdom* [1998] TLR 379.

A failure to give proper disclosure in the context of a trial may violate art 6 by preventing a fair trial: see *Edwards* v *UK* (1992) 15 EHRR 417 and *De Haes and Gijsels* v *Belgium* (1997) 25 EHRR 1.

Medical evidence

It may be possible for a person to rely on art 8 to refuse to undergo a medical examination or testing by the defendant. RSC O.25 r6 provides that the court has power to stay the personal injury action where the defendant has not been given a reasonable opportunity to examine medically the plaintiff. In future, perhaps, plaintiffs may rely on art 8 to restrict the scope and nature of medical examination, testing or treatment by defendants.

Video

Defendants often employ enquiry agents to video plaintiffs covertly hoping to catch the plaintiff acting in a manner which is incompatible with his alleged injuries. It is arguable that such activity contravenes art 8: cf *R* v *Brentwood Borough Council, ex parte Peck* [1997] TLR 676 concerning the lack of regulation of closed-circuit television in public places.

Unless orders

In *Canada Trust* v *Stolzenberg* [1998] New Law Digest 14 October the usual form of 'unless order', where a defendant is debarred from defending unless he complies with a previous order within a certain time, was not in breach of art 6(1). Such limitation of access to court pursues the legitimate aim of the efficient administration of justice.

Injunctions

It is arguable that Anton Piller injunctions and Mareva injunctions breach the Convention. In particular, there might be a threat to art 8 (the right to respect for home life) or art 1 of the First Protocol (the protection of property). In *Chappell* v *UK* (1988) 10 EHRR 510 the applicant's home was searched for pirate videos. However, the ECHR held that an Anton Piller order in respect of the applicant's premises did not violate art 8. Such limitation on his right to respect for home life pursued the legitimate aim of protecting others. It is likely that the domestic courts will consider that Mareva injunctions and Anton Piller orders do not in themselves violate the Convention but the potential for breaching the Convention, must be considered in all the circumstances of the case.

10 Privacy and Confidentiality

Introduction

This chapter concerns the complex interrelationship between two fundamental Convention rights – the right to privacy (art 8) and freedom of expression (art 10) – and looks at how their incorporation will alter national practice. Here privacy is considered in the traditional sense of control over personal information and freedom from intrusion.

These Convention rights assist applicants with conflicting interests: those claiming protection of their private life, and those, such as the media, who wish to publish information. An important question is whether the HRA will lead to a positive right to privacy under English law.

In Chapter 2 it has been noted that whilst art 10 holds a pre-eminent position within the Convention scheme, both art 8 and art 10 are qualified rights. Both may be limited in the interests of national security, the prevention of disorder or crime, the protection of health or morals and the protection of the rights and freedoms of others. Article 8 adds the further interest of public safety and the economic well-being of the country, while art 10 adds territorial integrity, the protection of the reputation of others, preventing disclosure of information received in confidence, and maintaining the impartiality of the judiciary.

Current privacy law

The current protection of privacy under English law is patchy and draws variously on:

1. the law of defamation;
2. malicious falsehood;
3. breach of confidence;
4. the Data Protection Acts 1984 and 1998;
5. the Protection from Harassment Act 1997; and
6. private nuisance (see Chapter 7).

It will be noted that, to some degree, these correspond to the exceptions in art 10(2).

85

Defamation

The law of defamation is, in principle, a legitimate limitation on freedom of expression under art 10(2). Injunctions to restrain publication and awards of damages on a finding of defamation clearly interfere with the freedom of expression. They are, however, capable of justification under art 10(2) on grounds of protecting the reputation of others. Whether in a given situation such restraints are justifiable will depend on whether they are 'necessary' and proportionate.

Factors of significance in determining whether an interference of this sort will be proportionate include: the nature, severity and duration of the restriction; the nature of the publication; its factual accuracy; and the relevance of the issue to public debate.

The ECHR has made clear however that prior restraint on publication (especially in newspapers) will require very careful scrutiny in view of the fact that delay in publication leads to news becoming stale: *Sunday Times (No 2) v UK* (1991) 14 EHRR 229. This sentiment is embodied in s12 of HRA, which will make it difficult to obtain prior restraints or gagging orders on an *inter partes* basis and virtually impossible to obtain *ex parte*.

The ECHR in the *Tolstoy* case (*Tolstoy Miloslavsky v UK* (1995) 20 EHRR 442) found the restraint on publication to be proportionate. The domestic courts had imposed an injunction restraining Count Tolstoy from accusing Lord Aldington of collusion in sending prisoners of war and refugees to their deaths by handing them over to Soviet forces at the end of the Second World War. The ECHR considered such an order necessary to prevent repetition of the defamatory allegations, the circulation of which was motivated at least in part by spite. The damages award, a record £1.5 million, was, however, considered disproportionate. The failure of domestic law at the time to ensure a sensible correlation between the level of damages and the injury to reputation suffered was thus a breach of art 10.

Attempts to restrain the publication of material which criticises politicians and concerns matters of genuine public debate are much harder to justify and will often breach art 10: see *Oberschlick v Austria* (1991) 19 EHRR 389 and *Lingens v Austria* (1986) 8 EHRR 103 (where a journalist was convicted of defamation for criticising the Austrian Chancellor).

In the recent disturbing case, *De Haes and Gijsels v Belgium* (1997) 25 EHRR 1, the ECHR considered the conviction of two journalists for allegedly defaming four appeal court judges to be disproportionate. A series of articles accused the judges of bias in a case where there was a wealth of evidence indicating that the father, a notaire, had been seriously abusing his children. The Antwerp courts refused to terminate the father's contact. Bias was alleged because the father and judges were all members of the same extreme right-wing organisations.

The ECHR accepted that preserving public confidence in the judiciary was a legitimate aim. It also noted that judges had a strong claim to privacy which required that they be 'protected from destructive attacks that are unfounded, especially in view of the fact that judges are subject to a duty of discretion that precludes them from replying to criticism.' The ECHR determined that the offending articles were based on a 'mass of detailed information' following thorough research, and stressed the journalists' duty to impart information on matters of public interest (which the public had a corresponding right to receive). In the ECHR's view this was particularly so in view of the seriousness of the allegations, which concerned both the fate of young children and the functioning of the system of justice in Antwerp.

Article 6 had also been violated in that there was a breach of the principle of 'equality of arms' because of the judges' refusal to allow the disclosure of evidence upon which the applicants sought to rely. The judges who were involved in the original custody case were thus placed at a very significant and unfair advantage in the defamation proceedings.

It is likely that the domestic law of defamation and the practice of the courts in applying it will generally comply with art 10. Whether it adequately protects privacy is, however, questionable: there are many invasions of privacy where a defamation action will not lie, for example where a story is true but intrusive and without public interest.

The disclosure of confidential information

In general domestic law complies with art 10 and protects confidential information. An action for breach of confidence is an important weapon in this armoury. Such an action requires that:

1. the information has 'the necessary quality of confidence about it';
2. the information has 'been imparted in circumstances importing an obligation of confidence'; and
3. there has been 'an unauthorised use of that information to the detriment of the party communicating it': *Coco v A N Clark Engineers Ltd* [1969] RPC 41.

In the words of Lord Goff in the 'Spycatcher' case (*Attorney-General* v *Guardian Newspapers (No 2)* [1990] 1 AC 109:

> ' ... a duty of confidence arises when confidential information comes to the knowledge of a person [the confidant] in circumstances where he has notice, or is held to have agreed, that the information is confidential, with the effect that it would be just in all the circumstances that he should be precluded from disclosing the information to others'.

Injunctions

An injunction is available to restrain disclosure or publication of confidential information except where there is genuine public interest in publication or the information is considered trivial. However, an injunction will not be granted to restrain re-publication of material which has lost its confidential nature.

The justification for injunctions imposed to protect confidential information are assessed by the ECHR in the same way as in relation to injunctions restraining defamation.

In *The Observer and The Guardian* v *UK* (1991) 14 EHRR 153 the applicant newspapers were prevented by interlocutory injunctions from publishing extracts from the book, *Spycatcher*, written by Peter Wright, allegedly in breach of his duty of confidentiality. The Attorney-General sought permanent injunctions. The interlocutory injunctions were imposed in June 1986 and were to last until October 1988. In July 1987 the book was published in the United States.

The ECHR accepted that the injunctions were a legitimate measure to maintain confidence in the judiciary (specifically to safeguard protect the Attorney-General's interest as a litigant pending trial) and to protect national security.

However, after publication in the United States, the injunctions were a disproportionate interference with press freedom. In reality, a significant minority of the ECHR considered the injunctions disproportionate from the outset. (See also *Sunday Times (No 2)* v *UK* (1991) 14 EHRR 229.) A smaller minority also criticised the ECHR's acceptance of the claim of national security without independent scrutiny. The ECHR refused to sanction the post-US publication injunctions, and noted the 'curious metamorphosis' whereby the purpose of the injunction had evolved, first, to protect the reputation of the secret service and, second, not to deter other former members from publishing their memoirs. Such objectives were sufficient to justify the continuation of the interference.

The protection of personal medical information

The ECHR has generally stood firm in protecting confidential medical information against disclosure to third parties, often balancing delicate public interest concerns.

For example, in the extraordinary case of *Z v Finland* (1997) 25 EHRR 371 the ECHR sanctioned the disclosure of the applicant's medical records in proceedings in which her husband was charged with rape and manslaughter for knowingly infecting his victims. The ECHR held, however, that disclosure by the court of her identity was a breach of art 8.

In *X v Y and Others* [1988] 2 All ER 648, the Queen's Bench Division adopted a similar approach. In that case, health workers passed to a national newspaper information from hospital records which identified two doctors as having AIDS. The health authority was granted a permanent injunction on the grounds that the public interest in preserving the confidentiality of hospital records identifying AIDS sufferers outweighed the public interest in the freedom of the press to provide such information, because victims of the disease ought not to be deterred by fear of discovery from going to hospital for treatment. Moreover, it was held, informed debate about AIDS could take place without publication of the confidential information in question. (See Chapter 3 on medical law.)

It is interesting to compare this with another case which does not concern medical records but other personal data, and did not give rise to an action for breach of confidence as the information was already in the public domain.

In *R v Chief Constable of North Wales, ex parte A and B* [1998] 3 WLR 57 two convicted paedophiles challenged the fairness of the decision taken by police to reveal details of their previous convictions to owners of a caravan site where they were staying. The result of this disclosure was that the two applicants had to leave the site which, in turn, led to the authorities losing contact with them. The Court of Appeal held as a matter of domestic law and under the Convention that the police were entitled to use the information if they reasonably concluded, having taken into account the interests of the applicants, that it was necessary to protect the public. In view of the approaching Easter holidays when many children would be on the site, the police had acted reasonably.

Reference should also be made to *Gaskin v UK* (1989) 12 EHRR 36 (see Chapter 4) where the applicant was able to defeat resistance to disclosure on grounds of confidentiality to gain access to social services records detailing his childhood in care. The applicant succeeded by relying on art 8 not art 10.

The protection of journalists' sources

Section 10 of the Contempt of Court Act (CCA) 1981 provides that:

> '... no person may require a person to disclose, nor is any person guilty of contempt of court for refusing to disclose, the source of information contained in a publication for which he is responsible, unless it be established to the satisfaction of the court that disclosure is necessary in the interests of justice or national security or for the prevention of disorder or crime.'

This provision was enacted in order to comply with the Convention. Notwithstanding, the ECHR still seems to places greater importance on freedom of expression than our domestic courts in the protection of journalists sources. The HRA may, of course, change this.

In *Goodwin* v *UK* (1996) 22 EHRR 123 the applicant had received information about the allegedly precarious financial position of a company which he intended to publish as a magazine article. The company obtained an injunction preventing publication, but wanted to identify who had stolen and leaked confidential documents to the applicant. The House of Lords (in *X Ltd* v *Morgan Grampian (Publishers) Ltd* [1991] AC 1) upheld a ruling that the protection of the journalist's sources under s10 of the Contempt of Court Act 1981 was outweighed by the interest of employer in identifying the source where a failure to do so might seriously damage his business (for example, if the information was passed to a competitor). The applicant failed to comply with the order for disclosure and was fined £5,000. This, he alleged, was a breach of art 10. The ECHR agreed, applying what was in essence the same test as the House of Lords but reaching the opposite conclusion, stating that the injunction provided sufficient protection and that the contempt order had a 'disproportionately chilling effect' on freedom of the press.

In *Camelot Group* v *Centaur Communications* [1998] 2 WLR 379 the Court of Appeal managed to distinguish *Goodwin* and in so doing arguably extended the s10 exceptions to permit the court to enforce disclosure so as to enable Camelot, the company running the National Lottery, to ensure the continued loyalty of its employees and ex-employees. The Court of Appeal was very critical of the disclosure of draft accounts indicating the salaries of the directors of Camelot. (For the employment implications for 'whistleblowers' see Chapter 5 on employment law and the Public Interest Disclosure Act 1998.)

The 1999 Rules of the Supreme of the Supreme Court (the White Book) state that the question of disclosure 'is to be determined in accordance with English law as set out in s10 and interpreted by the English courts in

X Ltd v *Morgan Grampian (Publishers) Ltd* (it being clear and unambiguous) and not therefore by the application of the decision of the ECHR in *Goodwin* v *UK* and the incorporation of art 10 of the ECHR in *Camelot Group* v *Centaur Communications*' (13A–28). It is very likely that the HRA will alter the substantive law on this issue, and will certainly alter the approach of the White Book editors.

Telephone tapping

As technology has advanced and methods of surveillance improved, the ECHR has stepped in to protect the individual against its abuse. *Malone* v *UK* (1984) 7 EHRR 14 is a high point of ECHR jurisprudence and led directly to enactment of the Interception of Communications Act (ICA) 1985.

In *Halford* v *UK* (1997) 24 EHRR 523 the police had intercepted the applicant's (the former Assistant Chief Constable of Mersyside) office telephone to obtain information to use against her in her sex discrimination claim against the force. Since the ICA 1985 did not apply to internal communications systems operated by public authorities, the interference with her private life and correspondence could not be justified as it was not 'in accordance with the law'. In addition to a violation of art 8, the absence of legal remedy also violated the applicant's rights under art 13. (See also *Kopp* v *Switzerland* (1998) 27 EHRR 91 where the tapping of a lawyer's telephones was found to violate art 8 on the grounds that the domestic law did not indicate clearly how the authorities' discretion was to be exercised.)

Where the employer is a private entity, rather than public authority, it is submitted that the ECHR should still find a violation where legislation is defective since this is a breach of the state's positive obligation under art 8.

Media intrusion

As the recent unsuccessful application (*Earl Spencer and Countess Spencer* v *UK* (1998) 25 EHRR CD 105) illustrates, this remains the most controversial aspect of the privacy/ freedom of expression debate.

The applicants complained about intrusion on their privacy when tabloid newspapers printed disclosures that Countess Spencer was receiving treatment for an eating disorder at a private clinic where she was photographed walking in the grounds, and implied that Earl Spencer's admitted adultery had contributed to his wife's psychological problems. The applicants complained that the UK had breached arts 8 and 13 by failing to prohibit publication and failing to provide a remedy whereby they could have prevented publication or claimed damages thereafter.

The Commission accepted the government's contention that the application was inadmissible due to the applicants' failure to pursue an action for breach of confidence and thereby exhaust their domestic remedies. The applicants maintained that breach of confidence was an inadequate remedy and an action on that basis would have been unlikely to succeed. In particular, they stressed that once the offending material had been published they could not rely on breach of confidence to prevent its re-publication. Further, they would have difficulty proving that the newspapers had had notice of the confidential nature of information, and moreover, it was questionable whether damages was an available remedy. Finally, there was no authority (other than obiter dicta) to support a claim that taking photographs could amount to a breach of confidence.

The Commission stated that whilst applicants do not need to exercise a remedy which does not offer 'any chance of redressing the breach' where there is doubt about the prospects of success, it 'should be submitted to the domestic courts for resolution'. It dealt with its decision in *Winer v UK* (1986) 48 DR 158, that the scope of the breach of confidence remedy was uncertain, by stating that since then the law of confidence in the UK had moved on.

Presumably the Spencers lost their appetite for litigation, so it is not known whether an action for breach of confidence would have succeeded. Even if it had, the fact remains that their case was highly unusual (they had proof of the identify of the informants), whilst in the majority of press intrusion cases breach of confidence cannot be established. There is rarely a prior relationship of confidence, and even if there is the rights of journalists to protect their sources makes it difficult to prove a breach of confidence. Further obstacles were referred to in the *Spencer* case above.

These shortcomings are graphically illustrated by *Kaye v Robertson and Another* [1991] FSR 62, in which the Court of Appeal considered the case of a a well known actor whose skull was shattered when part of a billboard fell through his windscreen in a storm. While he was in hospital recovering from surgery, journalists from the *Sunday Sport* entered his private room (ignoring notices prohibiting entry), interviewed him, took pictures and announced they would be publishing the interview as a 'scoop'. Mr Kaye (who had no memory of the 'interview') claimed that he had not consented to an interview and was in any event in no condition to consent, and sought an interlocutory injunction on the grounds of libel, malicious falsehood, trespass to the person (eg battery), and passing off.

The Court of Appeal considered that a claim for passing off was hopeless, taking a photograph with a flashlight could conceivably amount to a battery but was not strong enough to base an injunction on, and neither was an allegation of libel as it could not be said that a jury would certainly find that Mr Kaye had been libelled.

By straining the tort of malicious falsehood to prevent a 'monstrous invasion of his privacy', the Court was able to grant an injunction, although only in a limited form. Glidewell LJ appeared to express the views of all judges hearing the case when he stated that '[t]he facts of the present case are a graphic illustration of the desirability of Parliament considering whether and in what circumstances statutory provision can be made to protect the privacy of individuals'.

R v Brentwood Borough Council, ex parte Peck [1997] TLR 676 provides another example the current lacuna in the law. In that case the applicant tried to commit suicide by slitting his wrists with a knife. Film of him walking down the high street holding the knife was caught on closed circuit television and broadcast (and printed in the local paper). He was recognised by friends and neighbours.

Harrison J in the Queen's Bench Division held that the council was empowered by legislation to provide and operate closed circuit television to prevent crime, and that it was also empowered to distribute video recordings to the media so as to facilitate the prevention of crime. Thus, while the judge expressed sympathy with Mr Peck, he felt 'unable to conclude that the council had acted irrationally'.

Kaye is pending before the ECHR. However, to some extent the ECHR's decision may be superseded by developments following entry into force of the HRA. *Kaye* is only one example where the judiciary is poised to develop the common law to create an express right to privacy. When the Human Rights Bill was being debated in the Lords, the Lord Chancellor, for his part, said that he envisaged that the courts would be free to, and probably would, use the ECHR to develop the right to privacy in the common law. His expressed view was that to do this under the incorporated ECHR would have the advantage of requiring a balance between art 8 and art 10 rights. As the ECHR jurisprudence illustrates, this is no easy balance to achieve.

11 Education

Introduction

It would be tempting to read art 2 of the First Protocol and imagine that after the HRA comes into force the domestic courts will strike down many decisions by education authorities. In practice, although strongly worded, art 2 rarely provides effective relief. Often the domestic law is a more potent weapon for challenge. The UK has a reservation and accepts art 2 'only insofar as it is compatible with the provision of efficient instruction and training, and the avoidance of unreasonable public expenditure.'

Definition

The term 'education' is widely defined to include most aspects of influencing child development. It is distinct from teaching and is defined as '... the whole process whereby, in any society, adults endeavour to transmit their beliefs, culture and other values to the young, whereas teaching or instruction refers in particular to the transmission of knowledge and to intellectual development': *Campbell and Cosans* v *UK* (1982) 4 EHRR 293. Education does not extend, however, to vocational training.

Right to education

The draft version of art 2 which read 'Everyone has the right to education' was rejected as implying positive obligations on the state that were too onerous, perhaps extending to a duty to provide adult literacy courses or a particular standard of universal education. However, in spite of the negative wording – 'No person shall be denied the right to education' – art 2 protects a right to education: *Belgian Linguistic Case (No 2)* (1968) 1 EHRR 252. Although the education provided must not be useless, the Convention does not require the state to educate its children to any set minimum level or in any particular subjects. Nor is it the function of the ECHR to assess the quality of the education provided: *SP* v *UK* [1997] EHRLR 284. The article is primarily concerned with elementary education and will not guarantee university education for all: *X* v *UK* (1980) 23 DR 228. The state is free to establish selection criteria.

An individual's right to education encompasses: the rights of access to educational institutions existing at a given time; the right to an effective education; and the right to have official recognition of the studies a student has successfully completed: *Belgian Linguistic Case (No 2)*.

These rights are not absolute. The state may take into account 'the need and resources of the community and of individuals' but must not 'injure the substance of the right to education nor conflict with other rights enshrined in the Convention': *Belgian Linguistic Case (No 2)*. Given the negative obligation and the nature of the reservation, it is often easy for the state to defeat a challenge on the grounds of resources or the system of education: *Simpson* v *UK* (1989) 64 DR 188.

Also the state is not under a duty to finance education in private school or education at home.

Access to educational institutions existing at a given time

The right to education requires that individuals be allowed into schools. However, such right of access is not absolute. Parents may be required to educate their children at home in certain circumstances. The right of access to school is obviously relevant where children are excluded, suspended or withdrawn from school.

In *SP* v *UK* [1997] EHRLR 284 an intelligent five-year-old with a learning difficulty who was failing to achieve at school was removed from a succession of schools by his mother. The mother asked for a local education authority statement of special educational needs which was refused. He was then put in independent school, but eventually, because it was not able to provide the specialised requisite teaching, the boy was asked to leave. It was held that the applicant had not been excluded from the state educational facilities, as the mother had removed him to independent school. His access to state school had not therefore been violated.

Effective education

The right to education is meaningless unless the education available is effective. However, this does not mean that an individual is entitled to a particular level of education or particular assistance. The ECHR will not assess the quality of the education offered, beyond whether there was no effective education or not.

In *SP* v *UK* (above) the mother argued that teaching staff failed to take account of her child's special needs, particularly his short-term memory problems. In consequence, he had been unable to derive a positive benefit from his education which had contributed to his social and emotional problems, which, at ten years old, included suicidal tendencies. In relation to a statement of educational needs, the Commission acknowledged the wide measure of discretion left to the appropriate authorities as to how to make the best possible use of the resources available to them in the interests of disabled children generally. As the child's problems had worsened over time, it was not possible to conclude that it would have been right to statement him as having special educational needs at the age of five. There was, therefore, no violation of the Convention. In spite of the mother's claim that her son had not derived a positive benefit from his education, the ECHR determined that he had had an effective education. In contrast, under domestic law there is a duty to provide 'suitable education' which cannot be avoided by resource considerations: *R v East Sussex County Council, ex parte Tandy* [1998] 2 WLR 884.

Education in conjunction with the other articles of the Convention

Article 2 of the First Protocol must not be read in a void. Most notably art 8 enshrining the right to respect for private and family life, art 9 which protects freedom of thought, conscience and religion and art 14 which prohibits discrimination should be considered. In the *Belgian Linguistic Case (No 2)* (above) French-speaking parents in a bi-lingual area of Belgium did not have the right to an education in the language of their choice (being French) for their children. Such difference in treatment did not amount to discrimination and was not unlawful. Article 14 would, however, be violated if the entrance requirements for a particular school were discriminatory. Article 8 could be infringed if a requirement on parents to send their child away from home to be educated threatened family life.

Parents' philosophical and religious convictions

Definitions

The term 'respect' denotes positive obligation by the state. The state is forbidden 'to pursue an aim of indoctrination that might be regarded as not respecting parents' religious and philosophical convictions. That is the limit that must not be exceeded': *Kjelden, Busk, Maden and Pedersen* v

Denmark (1976) 1 EHRR 711. The term 'philosophical' was intended to encompass both ideological and non-religious beliefs and attitudes, but not language preferences *Belgian Linguistic Case (No 2)* (above). In *Campbell and Cosans* v *UK* (1982) 4 EHRR 293 'convictions' were defined as views that attained 'a certain level of cogency, seriousness, cohesion and importance'. The religions covered are 'known religions', which includes Jehovah's Witnesses: *Kokkinakis* v *Greece* (1993) 17 EHRR 397.

Purpose

Public authorities must not indoctrinate through their education system. There must be pluralism within the curriculum. The philosophical and religious convictions of parents must be respected.

The ECHR in *Valsamis* v *Greece* [1997] EHRLR 304 reaffirmed that 'the two sentences of art 2 [of protocol No 1] must be read not only in the light of each other but also, in particular, of arts 8, 9 and 10 of the Convention.'

Article 2 obliges the state to respect the parents' religious and philosophical convictions throughout state education programme, including during the performance of 'functions' assumed by the state, which include: administrative functions and even, for example, nationalistic parades as in *Valsamis* v *Greece* (above); discipline as in *Campbell and Cosans* v *UK* (above); and sex education as in *Kjelden, Busk, Maden and Pedersen* v *Denmark* (above).

The state is not allowed to indoctrinate pupils whether they attend state or independent schools. This does not mean that a teacher may not express opinions. After all, the freedom of expression is in itself a Convention right, albeit a qualified right. Moral or religious beliefs which contravene art 10(2) (namely those which threaten national security, territorial integrity, public safety, prevention of crime or disorder, protection of health or morals, protection of the reputation or rights of others, preventing the disclosure of confidential information, and maintaining the authority and impartiality of the judiciary) may be prohibited from being expressed.

In *Valsamis* v *Greece* (above) the applicant was a pupil who was a Jehovah's Witness committed to pacifism. She refused to participate in a school parade on same day as a military parade. As a result she was suspended. The ECHR reaffirmed that the applicant was entitled to respect for her religious convictions. However, in this particular case, the parade did not offend pacifist views. The ECHR took note of the parents' ability to enlighten and advise their children on their pacifist views. It is odd that the ECHR was prepared to rely on the parents' efforts to undermine potential indoctrination. Article 2 is aimed at preventing indoctrination and avoiding the need for the parents' efforts. Interestingly, the dissenting judges urged the ECHR to accept the applicant's subjective perception of the symbolism and significance of the school parade and its religious and philosophical connotations, unless they were obviously unfounded and unreasonable. The ECHR decided that it should form its own objective view. Again, this suggests that the parents' convictions are not paramount as is suggested in the wording of art 2.

However, if the state educates pupils on a particular topic in the public interest of a democratic society, in a manner which does not indoctrinate a particular religious or philosophical attitude, the ECHR will not interfere with such education. In *Kjelden, Busk, Maden and Pedersen* v *Denmark* (above) the parents did not want their child to receive sex education because of their religious convictions. However, because the state did not force any particular moral view, and it sex education was a topic in the public interest, the ECHR concluded that the state was acting lawfully. The suggestion that if the parents objected to sex education for their child the parents' remedy lay in removing their child to an independent school or educating the child at home is disconcerting.

If the domestic court considered that the availability of private school or home tuition negated the duty to respect the Convention in state schools art 2 of the First Protocol would be toothless.

12 European Community Law

Introduction

Over the past 30 years the European Court of Justice has, albeit with some initial reluctance, developed a distinct body of human rights law. This is important in two ways: first, because it offers the litigant in the domestic courts an alternative way to enforce its human rights other than via the Strasbourg machinery (and after spring 2000 via the HRA); and, second, because EC human rights law can be used to challenge the legality of acts of the EC institutions. The ECHR is not competent to do this, as the Community is not a signatory to the Convention, although its member states of course are. Indeed, the ECJ in Opinion 2/94 on *Accession by the Community to the European Convention on Human Rights* [1996] ECR 1–1759 ruled that the Community lacked the legislative competence to accede to it.

The ECHR does consider itself competent to examine all acts (and omissions) of the contracting states, including acts relating to the application of EC laws. This overlapping jurisdiction with the ECJ has caused problems, as will be seen in this chapter.

The general principles of Community law

The emergence of the rights

The Treaty of Rome set up an economic community and was not drafted with the aim of protecting human rights. However, in the late 1960s and early 1970s, the constitutional courts of some member states were refusing to accept that Community law could apply if it violated the fundamental human rights enshrined in their constitutions. Faced with this rebellious challenge to the supremacy of Community law, the ECJ took the expedient step of acknowledging that fundamental human rights formed a part of the 'general principles' of Community law.

The important case of *Stauder* v *City of Ulm* [1969] ECR 419 concerned a Community scheme to provide cheap butter to people on benefits. The applicant was a war veteran and objected to the requirement that he present a coupon with his name and to receive the butter was a humiliation which violated his fundamental human rights. He claimed that the Community measure was invalid in so far as it contained this requirement. The ECJ held that the measure did not require the applicant's name to appear on the coupon and so that 'the provision at issue contains nothing capable of prejudicing the fundamental human rights enshrined in the general principles of Community law and protected by the Court.' (See also *Internationale Handelgesellschaft* Case 11/70 [1970] ECR 1125.)

The ECJ then went on to recognise that in addition to the traditions of the member states, international treaties were a source of these fundamental human rights: see *Nold* v *EC Commission* Case 4/73 [1974] ECR 491. As has been noted, while the institutions of the European Union are not signatories of the Convention, the member states are. On this basis it was acknowledged in *Rutili* v *Minister for the Interior* [1975] ECR 1219 that the European Convention on Human Rights has a special role as a source of Community law.

Accordingly, all Community legislation is interpreted in the light of the Convention and the legality of acts of the Community institutions are judged so as to be compatible with it. This jurisdiction is, however, the exclusive province of the ECJ and not the ECHR.

Article F(2) of the Treaty of Amsterdam (which is not yet in force) further provides that 'the Union shall respect fundamental rights, as guaranteed by the European Convention for the protection of Human Rights and Fundamental Freedoms ... as general principles of Community law.'

The content of the rights

The existence of EC fundamental rights is thus clear. However, the content of these fundamental rights and other general principles can be difficult to discern.

In *Nold* v *EC Commission* (above) Nold, a coal wholesaler, complained that an EC Commission decision under the ECSC Treaty that coal wholesalers could not buy Ruhr coal direct from the selling agency, unless they agreed to purchase a certain minimum quantity, violated his fundamental rights. The ECJ appeared to acknowledge the existence of his right to property and his right to the free pursuit of an economic activity, but held that they were not absolute rights but were subject to limitations 'justified by the overall objectives pursued by the Community'. No infringement had therefore taken place.

Similarly, in *Hauer* v *Land Rheinland-Pfalz* Case 44/79 [1979] ECR 3727, the applicant complained that a Community regulation banning (temporarily) the new planting of vineyards violated these same rights.

Again, the ECJ acknowledged the existence of the rights but justified the measure in the general interest. In reaching this conclusion, the ECJ referred to the constitutions of three member states to establish that the right to property is subject to restrictions and also analysed the relevant provisions of the Convention.

A number of commentators (most notably Schermers, in 'The European Communities Bound by Fundamental Human Rights' (1990) 27 CML Rev 249 at 253–5, and Advocate-General Warner) consider that any right constitutionally protected in any one member state must, as a matter of law, be accepted as a fundamental right at the Community level. The ECJ does not, however, share this view, and what its jurisprudence indicates is that if a right is generally accepted throughout the Community and does not prejudice Community aims, the ECJ will probably adopt it. The position is different if the right is controversial. For example, in *Society for the Protection of the Unborn Child* v *Grogan* Case 159/90 [1991] ECR 1–4685 the ECJ refused to elevate the right to life of the unborn enshrined in the Irish constitution to a principle of Community law.

In spite of this uncertainty, there are a number of 'general principles' which are clearly established by the ECJ's jurisprudence. In addition to the right to property and the right to pursue a trade referred to above, such principles include:

- legal certainty;
- proportionality;
- legitimate expectation (derived from German law);
- equality;
- the right to a hearing; and
- legal professional privilege.

As with Convention rights, the scope and content of these rights constantly evolves as the need arises.

Application of these rights in competition law

Within the competition law field, these general principles have been applied and developed so as to curtail some of the very wide-reaching powers granted to the Commission by Council Regulation 17/62 implementing arts 85 and 86 of the EC Treaty (OJ English Special Edition 1959–1962, p87).

Rights of the defence

In one of the earliest cases, *Transocean* v *EC Commission* [1974] ECR 1063, the EC Commission had granted an exemption under art 85(3) to an anti-competitive agreement between members of the Transocean Marine Paint Association, subject to a condition that it be informed of any links between members and other companies or firms in the paint sector. The ECJ accepted the Association's contention that it had no advance notice of the intended condition and so no opportunity to submit its observations on it. The ECJ found a breach of an important procedural requirement and 'the general rule that a person whose interests are perceptibly affected by a decision taken by a public authority must be given the opportunity to make his point of view known.' Accordingly, it annulled the condition in issue.

By the mid 1980s the ECJ had consolidated its growing body of 'procedural requirements' and was able to articulate that 'the necessity to have regard to the rights of the defence is a fundamental principle of Community law': *Michelin* v *EC Commission* [1983] ECR 3461. It also began, for the first time, to interpret provisions of the Convention, while applying them with varying degrees of zeal.

Right against self-incrimination

In *Orkem* v *EC Commission* [1989] ECR 3283 Orkem refused to answer questions from the EC Commission in the course of an investigation into alleged price fixing in the thermoplastics industry. Orkem sought to annul the request on the grounds, inter alia, that it breached its privilege against self-incrimination. The ECJ acknowledged the EC Commission's wide investigatory powers, but held that it could not 'by means of calling for information, undermine the rights of the defence of the undertaking concerned'. Accordingly, the EC Commission was not permitted to 'compel an undertaking to provide it with answers which might involve an admission on its part of the existence of an infringement which it is incumbent on the Commission to prove' (paras 34 and 35). The offending questions which, for example, sought 'clarification' on 'every step or concerted measure which may have been envisaged or adopted to support such price initiatives', were therefore annulled.

In reaching its conclusion, the ECJ referred to art 6 of the Convention, but did not consider it of assistance on the basis that neither the wording of the article nor the jurisprudence of the ECHR indicated that it upheld the right not to give evidence against oneself.

Since then, the ECHR has developed this right. For example, in *Saunders* v

UK (1996) 23 EHRR 313, the ECHR found that in using answers which Saunders had been compelled to give to DTI inspectors under penal sanction as evidence in his criminal trial, the prosecution had violated his right to a fair trial under art 6(1). The ECHR emphasised that the right to silence and the right not to incriminate oneself 'lie at the heart of the notion of a fair procedure under art 6', and went on to hold that the right not to incriminate oneself cannot be confined to statements of admission of wrongdoing or remarks that are 'directly incriminating': see also *Funke v France* (1993) 16 EHRR 297.

In the light of these decisions, it may be that a future challenge to a request for information by the EC Commission will be found to violate an undertaking's rights under art 6. It is worth noting neither case was mentioned in the recent decision, *Otto v Postbank* [1993] ECR 1–5683, which was brought to the ECJ on a preliminary reference from The Netherlands.

The rule against bias

On several occasions undertakings have argued that the Commission's position as both plaintiff/prosecutor and judge in competition matters violates their rights under art 6 to an independent and impartial tribunal: *Musique Diffusion Francaise v EC Commission* [1983] ECR 1825; *FEDETAB* [1978] ECR 2111; and *Heintz van Landewyck v EC Commission* [1980] ECR 3125. The ECJ's response has been to rule that the Commission was not a tribunal within the meaning of art 6(1) and that the determination it conducted was administrative. This is a somewhat unsatisfactory conclusion, particularly given that the ECJ held in *Orkem* (above) that art 6 may be relied on by an undertaking subject to investigation under EC competition law. A more convincing argument in favour of conformity with art 6 is that the right of appeal, by which the Court of First Instance (CFI) has unlimited jurisdiction to review decisions of the Commission to impose fines, provides adequate protection.

Delay

Delays in the determination of competition cases before the CFI and the ECJ may prompt reliance on art 6. Under art 175 of the EC Treaty, a complainant can already bring an action for a 'failure to act', but art 6 might, in future, reinforce such claims.

Dawn raids

The Commission's conduct of 'dawn raids' (art 14 investigations) has also been challenged before the ECJ for compatibility with art 8 of the Convention. To date, the ECJ has refused to find any such violation: see

National Panasonic v *EC Commission* [1980] ECR 2033 and *Akzo* v *EC Commission* [1986] ECR 2585. In *Hoechst* v *EC Commission* [1989] ECR 2859 the ECJ considered the art 8 argument based on the 'inviolability of the home' and stated that 'although the existence of such a right must be recognised in the Community legal order as a principle common to the laws of the member states in regard to the private dwellings of natural persons, the same is not true in regard to undertakings ...' (para 17). The ECJ continued, 'the protective scope of that article is concerned with the development of man's personal freedom and may not therefore be extended to business premises. Furthermore, it should be noted that there is no case law of the European Court of Human Rights on that subject' (para 18).

Within three years this latter statement became false. There is now case law on the subject. *Niemietz* v *Germany* (1992) 16 EHRR 97 concerned the search of a lawyer's offices which was alleged to have been disproportionate to its purpose of preventing crime and protecting the rights of others. The ECHR held that the right to respect for private life extended to business premises, stating that 'to interpret the words "private life" and "home" as including certain professional or business activities or premises would be consonant with the essential object and purpose of art 8, namely to protect the individual against arbitrary interference by the public authorities' (para 31).

In three cases concerning French customs officials – *Funke, Miailhe* and *Cremieux* (at (1993) 16 EHRR 297, 322 and 357) – the ECHR considered in some depth investigating authorities' powers of search and seizure and held that such a powers can be justified under art 8(2), but that in order to be considered proportionate 'the relevant legislation and practice must afford adequate and effective safeguards against abuse.' In view of the fact that the French customs authorities had sole competence to assess the value, length and scale of inspections, and that there was no requirement for judicial authorisation, the safeguards were insufficient.

Given the striking breadth of the EC Commission's powers and comparative dearth of procedural safeguards, the dawn raid process may thus have become vulnerable to a challenge under art 8 on grounds of proportionality. Under the Competition Act 1998 a warrant is required for seizures from third parties, but not those reasonably suspected of anti-competitive behaviour. These powers may become equally vulnerable.

Choosing the HRA or Community law

The choice for an applicant whether to enforce a Convention right, or other general principle of Community law, through Community law or through the HRA will only arise where the national measure is adopted pursuant to Community law or in reliance upon it. The choice will clearly arise when a domestic court is required to interpret Community law, but the position is less clear when the domestic provisions in force or administrative action taken are only indirectly linked to Community law. Determining whether a measure is 'within the sphere of Community law' is a thus complex exercise.

A number of recent decisions have considered this conflict. In *R* v *Ministry of Agriculture, Fisheries and Food, ex parte Hamble Fisheries* [1995] 1 CMLR 533 Sedley J held that the general principle of legitimate expectation should apply to a fishing licensing regime since the purpose of the admittedly domestic measure was to implement the Common Fisheries Policy.

Arguably, the ECJ in the *Phil Collins* case ([1993] ECR 1–5145) went further and found that the general principles should bind member states in a very broad range of circumstances. However, this has not been followed in the recent cases decided in the English courts: see, for example, *R* v *Ministry of Agriculture, Fisheries and Food, ex parte First City Trading Ltd and Others* [1997] Eu LR 195.

Where an applicant has a choice, the Community law route will generally be preferable. The reasons for this are explained below.

An important difference is that the requirements of standing are broader under Community law than under the HRA. As will be seen in Chapter 13, to bring a claim an applicant must be a 'victim' in the sense of being 'directly affected' by the act or omission at issue. Where the complaint is made under Community law, the domestic rules of standing apply by reason of the principle of national autonomy. Given the increasingly wide approach to standing applied in the English courts, which commonly grant standing to public interest groups, this is a significant advantage of the Community law route.

The most important difference between the two routes is in the remedy which is available to an applicant upon breach. By virtue of the principle of the supremacy of Community law, a domestic court will disapply a provision (including a statute) which conflicts with Community law: *R* v *Secretary of State for Transport, ex parte Factortame (No 2)* [1991] 1 AC 603 and *R* v *Secretary of State for Employment, ex parte Equal Opportunities Commission* [1995] 1 AC 1. Under the HRA, however, a court will not have this power. The best it could do would be to declare the piece of legislation to be incompatible with the Convention. It would then be open to the relevant minister to amend the legislation, but there would be no obligation to do so (see Chapter 14).

There are further advantages to the Community law remedies regime. While member states are free to determine the remedies available for breaches of Community law, these remedies must be at least as generous as those provided for equivalent wrongs under domestic law. Further EC rights must be given 'effective protection': *Von Colson v Land Nordrhein-Westfahlen* [1984] ECR 1891. This is a very important requirement that has forced national courts to develop remedies where none had existed before so as to safeguard Community law rights: *R v Secretary of State for Transport, ex parte Factortame (No 4)* [1996] ECR 1–1029.

In summary, therefore, if a member state implements an EC directive in such a way as to breach the Convention, an applicant who suffers damage as a result will (provided he has standing) have a choice whether to challenge the legislation using the HRA or Community law. If he has suffered some financial loss he may be better off under Community law as he may have a *Francovich* damages claim if the breach is sufficiently serious: see *Francovich v Italian State* [1991] ECR 1–5357 and *Brasserie du Pêcheur SA v Germany* [1996] CMLR 889; [1996] ECR 1–1029. Given the Community law principles that damages must provide effective compensation, and an adequate remedy, the level of damages under *Francovich* may be higher than under the HRA which refers back to the notoriously ungenerous ECHR awards (see further Chapter 14).

It may also be that in some cases the grounds of review are wider under Community law. For example, the concept of proportionality is generally applied with greater rigour under Community law than by the ECHR. Also whereas the ECHR often falls back on the margin of appreciation argument to give contracting states leeway, a stricter test is applied in Community law when a limitation on a fundamental freedom is in issue. While under both tests the interference must be no greater than the minimum necessary to achieve the legitimate aim, the ECJ will often consider whether a less restrictive means was available to the authorities: see for an example picked at random the 'Danish Bottles' case (*EC Commission v Denmark* [1988] ECR 4607). Having said this, many commentators, and the Lord Chancellor, expect that the Community law and ECHR notions of concepts such a proportionality will merge once the HRA comes into force: 'The development of Human Rights in Britain' [1998] PL 221 at 231.

Before concluding the chapter it must be noted that the jurisdictional relationship between the ECHR in Strasbourg (charged with applying the

Convention) and the ECJ in Luxembourg (responsible for ensuring the uniform application of EC law) has always been unclear and uneasy. As seen above, the ECJ protects human rights by applying its self-styled general principles of law, including Convention rights, where the matter is within the scope of Community law. The ECHR has no competence to review the acts of the Community institutions but will rules on the acts of contracting states which relate to the application of EC laws.

In *Gerard Adams and Tony Benn v UK* (1997) 88A DR 137 Mr Adams challenged an exclusion order imposed on him under the Prevention of Terrorism (Temporary Provisions) Act 1989 that prevented him from entering the UK mainland. A preliminary reference was made by the High Court to the ECJ for a determination as to whether his right to free movement under art 8a(1) of the EC Treaty had been infringed. The ECHR was also seized and, for its part, was asked to determine whether the exercise of the right of free movement constituted a 'civil right' within the meaning of art 6. In the event, the exclusion order was lifted and the reference to the ECJ revoked on the grounds that the matter had become academic.

The Commission, surprisingly, did not decline jurisdiction but boldly ruled that the right of free movement, being of a public law nature, did not constitute a 'civil right'. The Commission reached its conclusion having regard to 'the origin and general nature of the provision' which it found to 'lack the personal, economic or individual aspects ... characteristic to the private law sphere'. Consequently, there was no right of access guaranteed. This conclusion, however, is difficult to reconcile with the ECJ's consistent view of the four fundamental freedoms (the right to free movement of goods, persons, services and capital) as economic rights pertaining to the individual. Bearing in mind the importance of these 'fundamental freedoms' in the EC context, it is difficult to image the ECJ holding an individual would not have access to a court to determine the legality of a restriction on his right to free movement.

As this case illustrates, the ECHR is reluctant to find that a contracting state has violated the Convention by implementing its Community obligations: see *Procolo v Luxembourg* (1995) 22 EHRR 193. The ECHR accordingly operates what has been called 'a low intensity review' of Community measures. In view of the fact that domestic courts cannot strike down EC measures (this being the exclusive preserve of the ECJ), the onus shifts to the ECJ to defend Convention principles in the application of EC law. The ECJ's jurisprudence (especially in competition cases) illustrates that. Unless the ECJ applies a strict level of scrutiny,

Community law will not be assessed for compliance with the Convention. Given the real doubts about democratic accountability in the adoption of Community legislation, this is a serious concern.

Many commentators have views on how this should be resolved. Fortunately, a conclusion on this is beyond the scope of this work!

13 Bringing a Claim under the HRA

In this chapter the procedure for relying on the HRA other than by way of judicial review (which is considered in Chapter 6) is examined.

The nature of the claim

A violation of Convention rights will be a new and independent cause of action. Section 6(1) HRA provides that a public authority must act in a manner which is compatible with the Convention. 'Act' includes a failure to act (s6(6) HRA) but does not include a failure to legislate. The public authority will have a defence if, as a result of primary legislation, the authority could not have acted differently; or where the public authority is required by legislation to act in a manner which is incompatible with the Convention (s6(2) HRA).

Where to claim?

An action against a public authority for acting in violation of the Convention may be brought 'in the appropriate court or tribunal'. This could be any court, and includes magistrates' courts, courts-martial, employment tribunals, county courts, the High Court, the Court of Appeal and the House of Lords. Obviously, points relating to the Convention which arise in the course of litigation already before a particular court will be dealt with by that court. For example, if procedural unfairness arises, such as excessive delay in breach of art 6(1), in an action before the county court, then the county court will rule on the issue.

In determining whether to bring an action against a public authority by way of judicial review or otherwise, a litigant must analyse whether the litigation concerns a matter of public law or private civil law in the usual way. Employment issues for example are not matters of public law and therefore should not proceed by judicial review. Actions involving private law against pure public authorities (see page 111) should be brought in the civil courts and not by way of judicial review.

Who can claim?

Section 7(3) HRA requires that 'the applicant ... is, or would be, a victim of that act'. In fact, the definition of victim is very wide. The statute expressly covers potential and actual victims. The HRA adopts the definition of 'a victim for the purposes of art 34 of the Convention if proceedings were brought in the [ECHR] in respect of that Act': s7(7) HRA).

A victim

Direct effect of breach of Convention

The ECHR considers a person to be a victim if he is directly affected by the unlawful act: so that, if a Convention right is breached and as a result he either suffers a detriment (*Klass v Germany* (1978) 2 EHRR 214 (para 33)), or might suffer a detriment (*Malone v UK* (1984) 7 EHRR 14 (para 64)), he is directly affected. A victim need not suffer actual detriment or prejudice. However, a mere theoretical threat or possibility of a detriment is insufficient: *Leigh, Guardian Newspapers Ltd and Observer Ltd v UK* (1984) 38 DR 74. It is a question of degree. There must be a 'reasonable likelihood' of suffering a detriment (*Hilton v UK* (1998) 57 DR 108) for a person to be directly affected.

If there is only a potential risk of violation of a Convention right, the threat of violation must be imminent: *Campbell and Cosans v UK* (1982) 4 EHRR 293 and *Soering v UK* (1989) 11 EHRR 439.

Indirect effect of breach of Convention

A person is a victim if they are affected in consequence of an unlawful act: for example, the wife of intended deportee (*Abdulaziz v UK* (1985) 7 EHRR 471); the widow of a terrorist victim (*Mrs W v UK* (1983) 32 DR 190); and the father of foetus facing termination: *Paton v UK* (1980) 19 DR 244.

Inherited actions

If an applicant dies in the course of an application under the Convention, his heirs will be permitted to continue the action.

Representative actions

Although rare, the ECHR will hear an application by a representative if the applicant is incapacitated. It will not hear a representative being a 'defender of the public interest': see *Klass v Germany* (1978) 2 EHRR 214 (para 33).

Participating in the actions of others

If potential litigants cannot qualify as 'victims' perhaps they can intervene in the actions of others. Public interest bodies could intervene to assist the domestic court either by providing evidence (as in *R v Ministry of Defence and Others, ex parte Smith and Others* [1996] 1 All ER 257) or by making written submissions. For example, in *Sheffield and Horsham* v *UK* (1998) 27 EHRR 163, when the domestic court was asked to allow a transsexual change to a birth certificate, Liberty filed written submissions regarding the legal recognition of transsexuals in comparative law. Alternatively, public interest groups may be allowed to argue important issues which the actual parties to the litigation refuse to take. In *Young, James and Webster* v *UK* (1981) 4 EHRR 38 neither party would argue that a closed shop was 'necessary in a democratic society', so the TUC did.

The HRA gives the government an express right to intervene in the applications of others, where the domestic court is considering making a declaration of incompatibility. Furthermore, the Lord Chancellor indicated that the domestic court would receive amicus curiae briefs in public interest cases: House of Lords debate, 24 November 1997, Hansard, col 832.

Who can be sued?

The HRA does not provide a comprehensive definition of a 'public authority'. It is only partially defined in s6(3) HRA and includes courts and tribunals, and persons exercising functions of a 'public nature'. It expressly excludes both Houses of Parliament (except the House of Lords sitting in its judicial capacity). A person is not a public authority subject to challenge under the HRA if only certain of his functions are of a public nature and the act complained of is merely private: s6(5) HRA.

The courts are left to crystallise the criteria for classifying a public authority. Some bodies, such as local authorities, are obviously public authorities ('pure public authorities'). Often a public authority will undertake the delegated responsibilities of the state or be an emanation of the state. Common features of public authorities are: the provision of a public service pursuant to measures adopted by the state; special powers to provide such a service; and such service being in the control of the state. If so, it is likely to be a public authority. A person may be a public authority if certain of his functions are of a public nature, but others are not (s6(3)(b) HRA) which are referred to as 'hybrid public authorities'.

No one knows which test the court will adopt to assess whether an entity is a public authority. There are a number of options: first, the approach of the European Court of Justice which adopts an 'emanation of the state' test; or, second, a definition following *Datafin* (*R* v *Panel on Takeovers and*

Mergers, ex parte Datafin plc [1987] 1 QB 814 (CA)); or, third, a completely independent and new test.

Public lawyers are familiar with applying the *Datafin* test in respect of bodies with some public law functions. A body is likely to be a public authority if the government would intervene in absence of such body, or if the government acquiesed or encouraged the activities of the body by underpinning its work or '[weaving] the body into the fabric of public regulation' or if the body exercises monopolistic powers in the public sphere (for example, sporting bodies) or if the aggrieved person agreed to submit to the jurisdiction of such a body (for example, licensing authorities). Examples of hybrid public authorities which exercise some public functions are the Legal Aid Board, the Financial Services Authority, Railtrack, the BBC, the Press Complaints Commission, the Bar Council and NHS trusts. Although it is impossible to predict with certainty, it is likely that the domestic court will adopt the *Datafin* test in order to determine whether a body is a public authority or not.

In relation to hybrid authorities, there is a distinction between public functions (requiring compliance with Convention rights) and private functions (which do not).

When can an action be brought?

An action under the HRA must be brought within one year of the act complained of occurring: s7(5) HRA. The court has a discretion to extend the primary limitation period if it considers an extension 'equitable having regard to all the circumstances'. However, any pre-existing shorter time limit (eg three months before employment tribunals) takes precedence. There is a potential argument under s11 HRA that an action for breach of the Convention may be able to benefit from the limitation period specific to the principal cause of action which is likely to be longer than one year.

How should it be pleaded?

It is not clear how an action against a public authority in respect of its act (or failure to act) in violation of the Convention should be pleaded. Perhaps it should be pleaded as a breach of statutory duty under s6 of the HRA, although given the negative wording of the statute, such pleading would be inelegant. Alternatively, following the New Zealand model, it should be pleaded as a breach of the Convention as a new independent cause of action. Again, this latter suggestion does not sit easily with the wording of the HRA but will be more readily comprehensible.

How can human rights cases be funded?

Of course if a litigant can afford to bring an action and pay for it personally, then there is not a problem. However, when a litigant cannot afford to fund his own litigation the situation is more complex. As yet there is no Human Rights Commission (akin to the Equal Opportunities Commission) which can sponsor litigation taking human rights points. A Human Rights Commission has not been ruled out entirely, but there are no current plans to establish one. Suggestions mooted for the future include a public interest fund for human rights litigation and power to the domestic court to award costs in civil litigation involving a public interest challenge similar to an order for costs 'out of central funds'. It is not thought that human rights litigation will be a popular area for litigation insurance.

Legal aid

In theory legal aid is available for human rights litigation. However, the usual test for the availability of legal aid is: (a) financial eligibility; (b) legal merits; and (c) reasonableness pursuant to the Legal Aid Act 1988. Such criteria are unsuitable for human rights cases. Unless a litigant is likely to receive significant damages, he may perhaps be refused legal aid because: first, the advantage gained would be 'trivial' (reg 29 Civil Legal Aid (General) Regulations 1989); or, second, the potential benefits do not justify the likely cost (Civil Legal Aid Notes for Guidance, para 7–03.4); or, finally, another person or group of people who do not qualify for legal aid has the same interest (Civil Legal Aid Notes for Guidance, para 7–03.35).

The Lord Chancellor has indicated that human rights cases will be considered differently when applications are made for legal aid. The criteria to be applied are unknown.

An absence of public funding may be itself a potential breach of the Convention in circumstances where the litigant needs public funding to litigate a violation of the Convention. However, such an assertion can be overstated. In *Andronicou and Constantinou* v *Cyprus* (1998) 25 EHRR 491 an armed and suicidal man was shot by security forces when they attempted to rescue his fiancée whom he was holding hostage. The applicants asserted that the absence of a formal legal aid system to bring civil proceedings against the security forces in respect of the deaths of the couple was in breach of the art 6 right to access to the court. An ex gratia offer of public funding to the applicants had been refused. The ECHR reiterated that it was not its function to dictate to a state what measures should be taken to guarantee an effective access to court. As funding had been offered, the applicants could not argue successfully that they had been deprived of an effective access to court by a lack of resources. The domestic court should examine the individual circumstances of the case. Sometimes the lack of legal aid will breach the right of access to the court, but the Convention does not establish an universal right to publicly funded litigation.

Pre-emptive cost orders

Such an order is made before the hearing of the matter and provides for a specified party to litigation to pay the costs irrespective of the outcome. It is highly unlikely that a litigant will be able to obtain such an order. The Court will use its power to make pre-emptive cost orders hesitantly. In *R v Lord Chancellor, ex parte the Child Poverty Action Group* [1998] 2 All ER 755 Dyson J cautioned that the discretion under s51 Supreme Court Act 1981 was appropriate:

> '... only in the most exceptional cases and, for such an order to be made in a public interest challenge case, it was necessary that the matters raised were of genuine general public importance and the merits of the claim were such that it would be in the public interest to make the order. The court should also take account of the financial resources of the parties and the amount of costs likely to be generated. The court would be more disposed to make an order where the respondent was plainly more able to bear the costs of the action than the applicant and where it was apparent that, unless an order was made, the applicant was likely to abandon the action and would be justified in doing so.'

The merest glimmer of hope of funding in the discretion of the court is possible. It should not, however, be relied upon.

14 Remedies, Relief and Damages

Section 8 remedies

If a s6 action results in a finding of unlawfulness, the courts have a broad discretion, pursuant to s8, to grant such relief as it considers 'just and appropriate'. It must be remembered that a public authority has not acted unlawfully if it was obliged by legislation so to act. The only limitation on the remedies available is that the court or tribunal in question must have the power to award the remedy sought. So, in judicial review proceedings, a court might award (inter alia) certiorari, mandamus or prohibition whereas an industrial tribunal could not. For their part, the criminal courts might order an acquittal or quash a conviction.

The most common remedy will, of course, be damages. The HRA provides in s8(3) and (4) that damages may be awarded where the court is satisfied that such an award is 'necessary to afford just satisfaction' to the person in whose favour it is made. In determining whether to award damages and/or the amount of the award, the court is required to take into account the principles applied by the ECHR in relation to the award of compensation under art 41 of the Convention.

The problem with applying the principles under art 41 is that such 'principles' don't really exist. Indeed, the ECHR is frequently criticised for its 'inconsistent and weak reasoning regarding the awarding of damages': see, for example, Alastair Mowbray 'The European Court of Human Rights' Approach to Just Satisfaction' [1997] PL 647.

In theory, at least, just satisfaction is awarded under three heads: pecuniary loss, non-pecuniary loss and costs and expenses. Pecuniary loss covers quantifiable financial loss consequent upon a violation. During a sample period from 1991 to 1995, pecuniary damages were sought in 22 cases and awarded in eight. Non-pecuniary damages (compensation for distress and anxiety) were sought in 24 cases and awarded in ten (although all these cases succeeded on the merits). In all other cases the ECHR considered that a finding of a Convention violation in itself was sufficient redress. The ECHR frequently reaches this conclusion in extradition and deportation cases.

Across the board the level of damages awarded is low. The ECHR never awards more than 50 per cent of the amounts claimed. By way of justification it has been pointed out that the ECHR's primary aim is to establish binding human rights standards, not to enrich applicants. Under the Convention, moreover, responsibility for providing redress for violations falls first to the national authorities.

The government's aim in referring to art 41 was almost certainly to keep the level of awards low. The domestic courts may or may not follow the ECHR practice in this respect. However, their methods of quantification are expected to be more scientific. To support an award for non-pecuniary damages, it may, for example, become the norm to adduce medical evidence as to the extent of an applicant's mental anguish.

Pecuniary damage

Principles

There must be a direct causal link between the violation and the loss and the loss must have actually been incurred: *Airey v Ireland* (1979) 2 EHRR 305. It is rare that a procedural failing, for example in breach of art 6, is considered to have caused pecuniary loss. The ECHR is usually reluctant to speculate on the outcome had a breach not occurred, and in the absence of reasonable certainty that the result would have been different without the violation, the claim is likely to be rejected: *Fredin v Sweden* (1991) 13 EHRR 784. The ECHR does not apply a loss of chance doctrine to award damages discounted by a percentage representing the loss of chance.

To some extent the 'weak reasoning' referred to above reflects internal disagreements within the ECHR about the correct methodology for assessment, for example, in the calculation of property values. In some cases the ECHR has admitted evidence from expert valuers. However, in other cases the it has made relatively large awards without any expert evidence at all: compare the cases *Papamichalopoulos and Others v Greece* (1995) 21 EHRR 439 and *Hentrich v France* (1995) 21 EHRR 199.

In *Lopez-Ostra v Spain* (1994) 20 EHRR 277 the ECHR found a violation of the applicant's right to respect for her home and private life by reason of severe toxic emissions. The applicant claimed damages under 5 headings:

1. £50,000 for distress suffered while living at home;
2. £12,000 for anxiety caused by daughter's serious pollution-related illness;
3. £10,000 for inconvenience caused by moving house;
4. £28,000 cost of new house;
5. £1,200 expenses in settling into new house.

The ECHR, however, concluded that 'the heads of damage do not lend themselves to precise quantification' and awarded a global sum of £16,000. This conclusion is surprising. Calculating the loss of value of a property by reference to its pre-and post-contamination values is an exercise the courts frequently conduct. Similarly, settlement costs should pose no difficulties in quantification. The ECHR's method of reaching its award remains a mystery.

Other examples of awards

In *Gaskin* v *UK* (1989) 12 EHRR 36 the denial of access to documents about the applicant's s about early life in care breached right to respect for private and family life. The applicant sought £380,000 in loss of earnings, alleging that his employment prospects had been injured owing to the loss of opportunities sustained by him. This was refused on the grounds that there was no causal link between the loss claimed and the violation, ie the non-disclosure of documents. The ECHR, however, awarded £5,000 non-pecuniary damages. The applicant claimed £117,00 costs and was awarded £11,000.

In *Open Door Counselling* v *Ireland* (1993) 16 EHRR 244 injunctions preventing the applicants from giving advice to women about procuring abortions violated their freedom of expression under art 10. One applicant (a non-profit-making organisation) claimed IR £62,172 for loss of earnings. The government objected and the ECHR awarded IR £25,000 'on an equitable basis'.

In *Young, James and Webster* v *UK* (1981) 4 EHRR 38 the applicants were dismissed from their jobs due to a closed-shop agreement found to violate their art 11 rights. They were awarded respectively £17,626, £45,215 and £8,706 for loss of earnings and travel privileges.

In *Pine Valley* v *Ireland* (1992) 14 EHRR 319 the ECHR found a violation of art 1 of the First Protocol and art 14 on the basis of an unlawful withholding of planning consent. The ECHR attempted an uncharacteristically reasonably scientific assessment of the loss suffered and awarded the applicants £1,200,000. This represented the value of the land if it had been immediately developed, less some reduction for rental value and difficulties in development attached to the land.

Non-pecuniary damage

Principles

Sometimes the ECHR will award a single, global figure under art 41 without distinguishing between pecuniary and non-pecuniary loss. It does not usually make awards for non-pecuniary loss to companies: *Manifattura v Italy* (1992) Series A 230–B. Numerous commentators have noted the apparently moral stance of the ECHR whereby it refrains from awarding damages to unsympathetic applicants, such as terrorists or convicted criminals. For example, in *McCann, Farrell and Savage v UK* (1995) 21 EHRR 97 the SAS operation in Gibraltar was found by a slender majority of the ECHR to have violated art 2, however, no damages were awarded.

The court does not usually award damages for extradition and deportation cases where the applicant risks ill treatment in breach of art 3 in the receiving state, for the reason that the application is anticipatory. The court can make an interim order suspending the proposed deportation: *Soering v UK* (1989) 11 EHRR 439 and *Chahal v UK* (1996) 23 EHRR 413.

Awards under this head are particularly opaque: the ECHR tends to assert that it has made an award 'on an equitable basis' but makes little attempt to explain or justify how it has quantified the award.

Examples of awards

Article 3

In *A v UK* [1998] TLR 578, a young boy who was beaten by his stepfather, who was acquitted on grounds of reasonable chastisement, was awarded £10,000 compensation for non-pecuniary damage and £20,000 legal costs and expenses.

In *Aydin v Turkey* (1998) 25 EHRR 251 the applicant was awarded £25,000 in respect of alleged rape and ill treatment while being detained by the gendarmerie.

Article 6

In *Konig v Germany* (1978) 2 EHRR 170 proceedings questioning the applicant's ability to run his medical practice had been pending for over ten years, forcing him to defer the search for an alternative career. He was awarded about £3,000 for anxiety and inconvenience.

In *Bock v Germany* (1989) 12 EHRR 247, where the applicant had to wait nine years for his divorce to go through, the ECHR awarded £4,000 (approximately).

In a series of cases where claims for compensation brought by people who contracted AIDS as a result of state-sponsored blood transfusion schemes took over two years to process, the ECHR ruled that particular expedition was required in the case of terminally ill patients and awarded payment of up to £20,000 to the victims (or to their families when the victim had died): *X* v *France* (1992) 14 EHRR 483; *Vallee* v *France* (1994) 18 EHRR 549; and *Karaka* v *France* [1994] Series A 289–B.

In *Helmers* v *Sweden* (Eur Court HR Series A 212–A) the applicant lecturer's claim for damage to his reputation under art 8, and discriminatory treatment under art 14, failed. However, he was awarded about £2,000 for having been deprived of the opportunity to put his claims before a court, bearing in mind the significant impact these issues had on his career and livelihood;

Article 8

In *McMichael* v *UK* (1995) 20 EHRR 205 the government resisted a damages award, arguing that it could not be asserted that the outcome of the care proceedings would have been different if the applicant has seen the undisclosed documents rather than having had them explained to her. The ECHR awarded £8,000 'on an equitable basis' accepting that some trauma, anxiety and feeling of injustice at the conclusion of the proceedings was due to the applicant's inability to see confidential documents.

In *Funke* v *France* (1993) 16 EHRR 297, where the applicant's home was unlawfully searched by customs and excise officials in connection with alleged exchange control offences, he was awarded £5,500.

In *Z* v *Finland* (1998) 25 EHRR 371 the disclosure of the applicant's HIV status was considered a serious violation of her right to privacy warranting an award of £22,000.

In *Guerra* v *Italy* (1998) 26 EHRR 357 the applicants were awarded £3,000 each in view of the failure of the authorities to provide information about the hazardous operations of a neighbouring pesticides factory.

Article 10

In *Halford* v *UK* (1997) 24 EHRR 523 the ECHR found the police's action in tapping the applicant's phone to obtain evidence against her in her sex discrimination claim was a serious violation and awarded her £10,000.

Cost and expenses which were incurred in domestic proceedings will be awarded if they are linked directly to the violation. Applicants have a much better chance of obtaining costs than of being awarded damages under the Convention

Declaration of incompatibility

It has been seen, in Chapter 1, that s3 of the HRA requires legislation to be interpreted so far as possible in accordance with the Convention.

Where this cannot be achieved, and there is an irreconcilable conflict between primary legislation and the Convention, an application may be made under s4 for a declaration of incompatibility. The Crown will be notified of such applications and may be joined to the proceedings. If granted, a declaration of incompatibility may lead to legislation to remove the incompatibility. This is a serious step for courts to take and is likely to be rare.

However, where a provision is declared incompatible, the minister has a wide discretion in deciding what action to take. Under s10(1)(b):

> '... if a minister of the crown considers that there are compelling reasons for proceedings under this section, he may by order make such amendments to the legislation as he considers necessary to remove the incompatibility'.

The choice of the term 'compelling reasons' is significant. The HRA could have obliged a minister to act, unless there were compelling reasons not to. In the absence of criteria to determine what are compelling reasons, this is an area where judicial review may be expected if ministers repeatedly find compelling reasons not to act following a finding of incompatibility.

Importantly, s6(6) provides that no liability will arise for failure to introduce or lay before Parliament any proposal for legislation or far a failure to make a remedial order.

The declaration of incompatibility – a sop to the principle of parliamentary sovereignty – has numerous shortcomings for the litigant. Most importantly, it does not affect the validity or operation or the enforcement of the provision in issue; and it is not binding on the parties to the proceedings in which it is made. Successful litigants may therefore have to wait a considerable length of time for the offending legislation to be changed, particularly where the proposed amendment is controversial. Whether an applicant could obtain a stay in such circumstances is questionable.

Petitioning the ECHR

The HRA will not entirely remove the prospect of litigation in Strasbourg. However, before making an application to the ECHR the applicant will have had to exhaust domestic remedies first, pursuant to art 26 of the Convention.

In effect, therefore, the HRA alters the admissibility criteria for applications to Strasbourg. Lawyers will have to raise Convention arguments in the national courts if they are not to find their applications to Strasbourg rejected. A failure to raise such arguments, could, therefore, leave an applicant without a remedy other than a claim for negligence against his legal advisers.

If the domestic route is tried and fails (for example, the domestic court refuses to apply a decision of the ECHR which determines an issue identical to the one before it) then, from the House of Lords, an application may be made to Strasbourg. Such applications will be heard by the newly incorporated European Court of Human Rights.

In this context, it is also important to note the requirements of art 13:

> 'Everyone whose rights and freedoms as set forth in the Convention are violated shall have an effective remedy before a national authority notwithstanding that the violation has been committed by persons acting in an official capacity.'

The Lord Chancellor has stated the government's purpose in excluding this provision from incorporation, namely to discourage the creation of new remedies when the existing array available under s8 (damages, declarations, certiorari etc) are considered adequate. However, in spite of non-incorporation, the government is still under an obligation pursuant to art 13 to provide a sufficient remedy. It is possible that obstacles preventing litigants coming to court to seek a remedy for violation of a Convention right will breach this article and prompt an application direct to Strasbourg. Possible obstacles may include the substitution of contingency fees for legal aid which is inappropriate to this type of litigation which involves cases that are inherently uncertain and where damages may not be sought. Even if damages are sought, they will probably be so low as to fail to attract any solicitor to the case.

In any event, it is doubtful whether the government's aim to curtail the forging of new remedies will be successful. It has made clear that in applying s8 HRA judges are entitled to (and indeed ought to) have regard to art 13 and its accompanying jurisprudence. The fun begins.

Appendix: the Human Rights Act 1998

Introduction

1 The Convention Rights

(1) In this Act 'the Convention rights' means the rights and fundamental freedoms set out in –

(a) Articles 2 to 12 and 14 of the Convention,

(b) Articles 1 to 3 of the First Protocol, and

(c) Articles 1 and 2 of the Sixth Protocol,

as read with Articles 16 to 18 of the Convention.

(2) Those Articles are to have effect for the purposes of this Act subject to any designated derogation or reservation (as to which see sections 14 and 15).

(3) The Articles are set out in Schedule 1.

(4) The Secretary of State may by order make such amendments to this Act as he considers appropriate to reflect the effect, in relation to the United Kingdom, of a protocol.

(5) In subsection (4) 'protocol' means a protocol to the Convention –

(a) which the United Kingdom has ratified; or

(b) which the United Kingdom has signed with a view to ratification.

(6) No amendment may be made by an order under subsection (4) so as to come into force before the protocol concerned is in force in relation to the United Kingdom.

2 Interpretation of Convention rights

(1) A court or tribunal determining a question which has arisen in connection with a Convention right must take into account any –

(a) judgment, decision, declaration or advisory opinion of the European Court of Human Rights,

(b) opinion of the Commission given in a report adopted under Article 31 of the Convention,

(c) decision of the Commission in connection with Article 26 or 27(2) of the Convention, or

(d) decision of the Committee of Ministers taken under Article 46 of the Convention, whenever made or given, so far as, in the opinion of the court or tribunal, it is relevant to the proceedings in which that question has arisen.

(2) Evidence of any judgment, decision, declaration or opinion of which account may have to be taken under this section is to be given in proceedings before any court or tribunal in such manner as may be provided by rules.

(3) In this section 'rules' means rules of court or, in the case of proceedings before a tribunal, rules made for the purposes of this section –

(a) by the Lord Chancellor or the Secretary of State, in relation to any proceedings outside Scotland;

(b) by the Secretary of State, in relation to proceedings in Scotland; or

(c) by a Northern Ireland department, in relation to proceedings before a tribunal in Northern Ireland –

(i) which deals with transferred matters; and

(ii) for which no rules made under paragraph (a) are in force.

Legislation

3 Interpretation of Legislation

(1) So far as it is possible to do so, primary legislation and subordinate legislation must be read and given effect in a way which is compatible with the Convention rights.

(2) This section –

(a) applies to primary legislation and subordinate legislation whenever enacted;

(b) does not affect the validity, continuing operation or enforcement of any incompatible primary legislation; and

(c) does not affect the validity, continuing operation or enforcement of any incompatible subordinate legislation if (disregarding any possibility of revocation) primary legislation prevents removal of the incompatibility.

4 Declaration of incompatibility

(1) Subsection (2) applies in any proceedings in which a court determines whether a provision of primary legislation is compatible with a Convention right.

(2) If the court is satisfied that the provision is incompatible with a Convention right, it may make a declaration of that incompatibility.

(3) Subsection (4) applies in any proceedings in which a court determines

whether a provision of subordinate legislation, made in the exercise of a power conferred by primary legislation, is compatible with a Convention right.

(4) If the court is satisfied –

(a) that the provision is incompatible with a Convention right, and

(b) that (disregarding any possibility of revocation) the primary legislation concerned prevents removal of the incompatibility,

it may make a declaration of that incompatibility.

(5) In this section 'court' means –

(a) the House of Lords;

(b) the Judicial Committee of the Privy Council;

(c) the Courts-Martial Appeal Court;

(d) in Scotland, the High Court of Justiciary sitting otherwise than as a trial court or the Court of Session;

(e) in England and Wales or Northern Ireland, the High Court or the Court of Appeal.

(6) A declaration under this section ('a declaration of incompatibility') –

(a) does not affect the validity, continuing operation or enforcement of the provision in respect of which it is given; and

(b) is not binding on the parties to the proceedings in which it is made.

5 Right of Crown to intervene

(1) Where a court is considering whether to make a declaration of incompatibility, the Crown is entitled to notice in accordance with rules of court.

(2) In any case to which subsection (1) applies –

(a) a Minister of the Crown (or a person nominated by him),

(b) a member of the Scottish Executive,

(c) a Northern Ireland Minister,

(d) a Northern Ireland department,

is entitled, on giving notice in accordance with rules of court, to be joined as a party to the proceedings.

(3) Notice under subsection (2) may be given at any time during the proceedings.

(4) A person who has been made a party to criminal proceedings (other than in Scotland) as the result of a notice under subsection (2) may, with

leave, appeal to the House of Lords against any declaration of incompatibility made in the proceedings.

(5) In subsection (4) –

'criminal proceedings' includes all proceedings before the Courts-Martial Appeal Court; and

'leave' means leave granted by the court making the declaration of incompatibility or by the House of Lords.

Public authorities

6 Acts of public authorities

(1) It is unlawful for a public authority to act in a way which is incompatible with a Convention right.

(2) Subsection (1) does not apply to an act if –

(a) as the result of one or more provisions of primary legislation, the authority could not have acted differently; or

(b) in the case of one or more provisions of, or made under, primary legislation which cannot be read or given effect in a way which is compatible with the Convention rights, the authority was acting so as to give effect to or enforce those provisions.

(3) In this section 'public authority' includes –

(a) a court or tribunal, and

(b) any person certain of whose functions are functions of a public nature,

but does not include either House of Parliament or a person exercising functions in connection with proceedings in Parliament.

(4) In subsection (3) 'Parliament' does not include the House of Lords in its judicial capacity.

(5) In relation to a particular act, a person is not a public authority by virtue only of subsection (3)(b) if the nature of the act is private.

(6) 'An act' includes a failure to act but does not include a failure to –

(a) introduce in, or lay before, Parliament a proposal for legislation; or

(b) make any primary legislation or remedial order.

7 Proceedings

(1) A person who claims that a public authority has acted (or proposes to act) in a way which is made unlawful by section 6(1) may –

(a) bring proceedings against the authority under this Act in the appropriate court or tribunal, or

(b) rely on the Convention right or rights concerned in any legal proceedings,

but only if he is (or would be) a victim of the unlawful act.

(2) In subsection (1)(a) 'appropriate court or tribunal' means such court or tribunal as may be determined in accordance with rules; and proceedings against an authority include a counterclaim or similar proceeding.

(3) If the proceedings are brought on an application for judicial review, the applicant is to be taken to have a sufficient interest in relation to the unlawful act only if he is, or would be, a victim of that act.

(4) If the proceedings are made by way of a petition for judicial review in Scotland, the applicant shall be taken to have title and interest to sue in relation to the unlawful act only if he is, or would be, a victim of that act.

(5) Proceedings under subsection (1)(a) must be brought before the end of –

(a) the period of one year beginning with the date on which the act complained of took place; or

(b) such longer period as the court or tribunal considers equitable having regard to all the circumstances,

but that is subject to any rule imposing a stricter time limit in relation to the procedure in question.

(6) In subsection (1)(b) 'legal proceedings' includes –

(a) proceedings brought by or at the instigation of a public authority; and

(b) an appeal against the decision of a court or tribunal.

(7) For the purposes of this section, a person is a victim of an unlawful act only if he would be a victim for the purposes of Article 34 of the Convention if proceedings were brought in the European Court of Human Rights in respect of that act.

(8) Nothing in this Act creates a criminal offence.

(9) In this section 'rules' means –

(a) in relation to proceedings before a court or tribunal outside Scotland, rules made by the Lord Chancellor or the Secretary of State for the purposes of this section or rules of court,

(b) in relation to proceedings before a court or tribunal in Scotland, rules made by the Secretary of State for those purposes,

(c) in relation to proceedings before a tribunal in Northern Ireland –

(i) which deals with transferred matters; and

(ii) for which no rules made under paragraph (a) are in force, rules made by a Northern Ireland department for those purposes,

and includes provision made by order under section 1 of the Courts and Legal Services Act 1990.

(10) In making rules, regard must be had to section 9.

(11) The Minister who has power to make rules in relation to a particular tribunal may, to the extent he considers it necessary to ensure that the tribunal can provide an appropriate remedy in relation to an act (or proposed act) of a public authority which is (or would be) unlawful as a result of section 6(1), by order add to –

(a) the relief or remedies which the tribunal may grant; or

(b) the grounds on which it may grant any of them.

(12) An order made under subsection (11) may contain such incidental, supplemental, consequential or transitional provision as the Minister making it considers appropriate.

(13) 'The Minister' includes the Northern Ireland department concerned.

8 Judicial remedies

(1) In relation to any act (or proposed act) of a public authority which the court finds is (or would be) unlawful, it may grant such relief or remedy, or make such order, within its powers as it considers just and appropriate.

(2) But damages may be awarded only by a court which has power to award damages, or to order the payment of compensation, in civil proceedings.

(3) No award of damages is to be made unless, taking account of all the circumstances of the case, including –

(a) any other relief or remedy granted, or order made, in relation to the act in question (by that or any other court), and

(b) the consequences of any decision (of that or any other court) in respect of that act,

the court is satisfied that the award is necessary to afford just satisfaction to the person in whose favour it is made.

(4) In determining –

(a) whether to award damages, or

(b) the amount of an award,

the court must take into account the principles applied by the European Court of Human Rights in relation to the award of compensation under Article 41 of the Convention.

(5) A public authority against which damages are awarded is to be treated –

(a) in Scotland, for the purposes of section 3 of the Law Reform (Miscellaneous Provisions) (Scotland) Act 1940 as if the award were made in an action of damages in which the authority has been found liable in respect of loss or damage to the person to whom the award is made;

(b) for the purposes of the Civil Liability (Contribution) Act 1978 as liable in respect of damage suffered by the person to whom the award is made.

(6) In this section –

'court' includes a tribunal;

'damages' means damages for an unlawful act of a public authority; and

'unlawful' means unlawful under section 6(1).

9 Judicial acts

(1) Proceedings under section 7(1)(a) inrespect of a judicial act may be brought only –

(a) by exercising a right of appeal;

(b) on an application (in Scotland a petition) for judicial review; or

(c) in such other forum as may be prescribed by rules.

(2) That does not affect any rule of law which prevents a court from being the subject of judicial review.

(3) In proceedings under this Act in respect of a judicial act done in good faith, damages may not be awarded otherwise than to compensate a person to the extent required by Article 5(5) of the Convention.

(4) An award of damages permitted by subsection (3) is to be made against the Crown; but no award may be made unless the appropriate person, if not a party to the proceedings, is joined.

(5) In this section –

'appropriate person' means the Minister responsible for the court concerned, or a person or government department nominated by him;

'court' includes a tribunal;

'judge' includes a member of a tribunal, a justice of the peace and a clerk or other officer entitled to exercise the jurisdiction of a court;

'judicial act' means a judicial act of a court and includes an act done on the instructions, or on behalf, of a judge; and

'rules' has the same meaning as in section 7(9).

Remedial action

10 Power to take remedial action

(1) This section applies if –

(a) a provision of legislation has been declared under section 4 to be incompatible with a Convention right and, if an appeal lies –

(i) all persons who may appeal have stated in writing that they do not intend to do so;

(ii) the time for bringing an appeal has expired and no appeal has been brought within that time; or

(iii) an appeal brought within that time has been determined or abandoned; or

(b) it appears to a Minister of the Crown or Her Majesty in Council that, having regard to a finding of the European Court of Human Rights made after the coming into force of this section in proceedings against the United Kingdom, a provision of legislation is incompatible with an obligation of the United Kingdom arising from the Convention.

(2) If a Minister of the Crown considers that there are compelling reasons for proceeding under this section, he may by order make such amendments to the legislation as he considers necessary to remove the incompatibility.

(3) If, in the case of subordinate legislation, a Minister of the Crown considers –

(a) that it is necessary to amend the primary legislation under which the subordinate legislation in question was made, in order to enable the incompatibility to be removed, and

(b) that there are compelling reasons for proceeding under this section,

he may by order make such amendments to the primary legislation as he considers necessary.

(4) This section also applies where the provision in question is in subordinate legislation and has been quashed, or declared invalid, by reason of incompatibility with a Convention right and the Minister proposes to proceed under paragraph 2(b) of Schedule 2.

(5) If the legislation is an Order in Council, the power conferred by subsection (2) or (3) is exercisable by Her Majesty in Council.

(6) In this section 'legislation' does not include a Measure of the Church Assembly or of the General Synod of the Church of England.

(7) Schedule 2 makes further provision about remedial orders.

Other rights and proceedings

11 Safeguard for existing human rights

A person's reliance on a Convention right does not restrict –

(a) any other right or freedom conferred on him by or under any law having effect in any part of the United Kingdom; or

(b) his right to make any claim or bring any proceedings which he could make or bring apart from sections 7 to 9.

12 Freedom of expression

(1) This section applies if a court is considering whether to grant any relief which, if granted, might affect the exercise of the Convention right to freedom of expression.

(2) If the person against whom the application for relief is made ('the respondent') is neither present nor represented, no such relief is to be granted unless the court is satisfied –

(a) that the applicant has taken all practicable steps to notify the respondent; or

(b) that there are compelling reasons why the respondent should not be notified.

(3) No such relief is to be granted so as to restrain publication before trial unless the court is satisfied that the applicant is likely to establish that publication should not be allowed.

(4) The court must have particular regard to the importance of the Convention right to freedom of expression and, where the proceedings relate to material which the respondent claims, or which appears to the court, to be journalistic, literary or artistic material (or to conduct connected with such material), to –

(a) the extent to which –

(i) the material has, or is about to, become available to the public; or

(ii) it is, or would be, in the public interest for the material to be published;

(b) any relevant privacy code.

(5) In this section –

'court' includes a tribunal; and

'relief' includes any remedy or order (other than in criminal proceedings).

13 Freedom of thought, conscience and religion

(1) If a court's determination of any question arising under this Act might affect the exercise by a religious organisation (itself or its members collectively) of the Convention right to freedom of thought, conscience and religion, it must have particular regard to the importance of that right.

(2) In this section 'court' includes a tribunal.

Derogations and reservations

14 Derogations

(1) In this Act 'designated derogation' means –

(a) the United Kingdom's derogation from Article 5(3) of the Convention; and

(b) any derogation by the United Kingdom from an Article of the Convention, or of any protocol to the Convention, which is designated for the purposes of this Act in an order made by the Secretary of State.

(2) The derogation referred to in subsection (1)(a) is set out in Part I of Schedule 3.

(3) If a designated derogation is amended or replaced it ceases to be a designated derogation.

(4) But subsection (3) does not prevent the Secretary of State from exercising his power under subsection (1)(b) to make a fresh designation order in respect of the Article concerned.

(5) The Secretary of State must by order make such amendments to Schedule 3 as he considers appropriate to reflect –

(a) any designation order; or

(b) the effect of subsection (3).

(6) A designation order may be made in anticipation of the making by the United Kingdom of a proposed derogation.

15 Reservations

(1) In this Act 'designated reservation' means –

(a) the United Kingdom's reservation to Article 2 of the First Protocol to the Convention; and

(b) any other reservation by the United Kingdom to an Article of the Convention, or of any protocol to the Convention, which is designated for the purposes of this Act in an order made by the Secretary of State.

(2) The text of the reservation referred to in subsection (1)(a) is set out in Part II of Schedule 3.

(3) If a designated reservation is withdrawn wholly or in part it ceases to be a designated reservation.

(4) But subsection (3) does not prevent the Secretary of State from exercising his power under subsection (1)(b) to make a fresh designation order in respect of the Article concerned.

(5) The Secretary of State must by order make such amendments to this Act as he considers appropriate to reflect –

(a) any designation order; or

(b) the effect of subsection (3).

16 Period for which designated derogations have effect

(1) If it has not already been withdrawn by the United Kingdom, a designated derogation ceases to have effect for the purposes of this Act –

(a) in the case of the derogation referred to in section 14(1)(a), at the end of the period of five years beginning with the date on which section 1(2) came into force;

(b) in the case of any other derogation, at the end of the period of five years beginning with the date on which the order designating it was made.

(2) At any time before the period –

(a) fixed by subsection (1)(a) or (b), or

(b) extended by an order under this subsection,

comes to an end, the Secretary of State may by order extend it by a further period of five years.

(3) An order under section 14(1)(b) ceases to have effect at the end of the period for consideration, unless a resolution has been passed by each House approving the order.

(4) Subsection (3) does not affect –

(a) anything done in reliance on the order; or

(b) the power to make a fresh order under section 14(1)(b).

(5) In subsection (3) 'period for consideration' means the period of forty days beginning with the day on which the order was made.

(6) In calculating the period for consideration, no account is to be taken of any time during which –

(a) Parliament is dissolved or prorogued; or

(b) both Houses are adjourned for more than four days.

(7) If a designated derogation is withdrawn by the United Kingdom, the Secretary of State must by order make such amendments to this Act as he considers are required to reflect that withdrawal.

17 Periodic review of designated reservations

(1) The appropriate Minister must review the designated reservation referred to in section 15(1)(a) –

(a) before the end of the period of five years beginning with the date on which section 1(2) came into force; and

(b) if that designation is still in force, before the end of the period of five years beginning with the date on which the last report relating to it was laid under subsection (3).

(2) The appropriate Minister must review each of the other designated reservations (if any) –

(a) before the end of the period of five years beginning with the date on which the order designating the reservation first came into force; and

(b) if the designation is still in force, before the end of the period of five years beginning with the date on which the last report relating to it was laid under subsection (3).

(3) The Minister conducting a review under this section must prepare a report on the result of the review and lay a copy of it before each House of Parliament.

Judges of the European Court of Human Rights

18 Appointment to European Court of Human Rights

(1) In this section 'judicial office' means the office of –

(a) Lord Justice of Appeal, Justice of the High Court or Circuit judge, in England and Wales;

(b) judge of the Court of Session or sheriff, in Scotland;

(c) Lord Justice of Appeal, judge of the High Court or county court judge, in Northern Ireland.

(2) The holder of a judicial office may become a judge of the European Court of Human Rights ('the Court') without being required to relinquish his office.

(3) But he is not required to perform the duties of his judicial office while he is a judge of the Court.

(4) In respect of any period during which he is a judge of the Court –

(a) a Lord Justice of Appeal or Justice of the High Court is not to count as a judge of the relevant court for the purposes of section 2(1) or 4(1) of the Supreme Court Act 1981 (maximum number of judges) nor as a judge of the Supreme Court for the purposes of section 12(1) to (6) of that Act (salaries etc);

(b) a judge of the Court of Session is not to count as a judge of that court for the purposes of section 1(1) of the Court of Session Act 1988 (maximum number of judges) or of section 9(1)(c) of the Administration of Justice Act 1973 ('the 1973 Act') (salaries etc);

(c) a Lord Justice of Appeal or judge of the High Court in Northern Ireland is not to count as a judge of the relevant court for the purposes of section 2(1) or 3(1) of the Judicature (Northern Ireland) Act 1978 (maximum number of judges) nor as a judge of the Supreme Court of Northern Ireland for the purposes of section 9(1)(d) of the 1973 Act (salaries etc);

(d) a Circuit judge is not to count as such for the purposes of section 18 of the Courts Act 1971 (salaries etc);

(e) a sheriff is not to count as such for the purposes of section 14 of the Sheriff Courts (Scotland) Act 1907 (salaries etc);

(f) a county court judge of Northern Ireland is not to count as such for the purposes of section 106 of the County Courts Act Northern Ireland) 1959 (salaries etc).

(5) If a sheriff principal is appointed a judge of the Court, section 11(1) of the Sheriff Courts (Scotland) Act 1971 (temporary appointment of sheriff principal) applies, while he holds that appointment, as if his office is vacant.

(6) Schedule 4 makes provision about judicial pensions in relation to the holder of a judicial office who serves as a judge of the Court.

(7) The Lord Chancellor or the Secretary of State may by order make such transitional provision (including, in particular, provision for a temporary increase in the maximum number of judges) as he considers appropriate in relation to any holder of a judicial office who has completed his service as a judge of the Court.

Parliamentary procedure

19 Statements of compatibility

(1) A Minister of the Crown in charge of a Bill in either House of Parliament must, before Second Reading of the Bill –

(a) make a statement to the effect that in his view the provisions of the Bill are compatible with the Convention rights ('a statement of compatibility'); or

(b) make a statement to the effect that although he is unable to make a statement of compatibility the government nevertheless wishes the House to proceed with the Bill.

(2) The statement must be in writing and be published in such manner as the Minister making it considers appropriate.

Supplemental

20 Orders etc under this Act

(1) Any power of a Minister of the Crown to make an order under this Act is exercisable by statutory instrument.

(2) The power of the Lord Chancellor or the Secretary of State to make rules (other than rules of court) under section 2(3) or 7(9) is exercisable by statutory instrument.

(3) Any statutory instrument made under section 14, 15 or 16(7) must be laid before Parliament.

(4) No order may be made by the Lord Chancellor or the Secretary of State under section 1(4), 7(11) or 16(2) unless a draft of the order has been laid before, and approved by, each House of Parliament.

(5) Any statutory instrument made under section 18(7) or Schedule 4, or to which subsection (2) applies, shall be subject to annulment in pursuance of a resolution of either House of Parliament.

(6) The power of a Northern Ireland department to make –

(a) rules under section 2(3)(c) or 7(9)(c), or

(b) an order under section 7(11),

is exercisable by statutory rule for the purposes of the Statutory Rules (Northern Ireland) Order 1979.

(7) Any rules made under section 2(3)(c) or 7(9)(c) shall be subject to negative resolution; and section 41(6) of the Interpretation Act Northern Ireland) 1954 (meaning of 'subject to negative resolution') shall apply as if the power to make the rules were conferred by an Act of the Northern Ireland Assembly.

(8) No order may be made by a Northern Ireland department under section 7(11) unless a draft of the order has been laid before, and approved by, the Northern Ireland Assembly.

21 Interpretation, etc

(1) In this Act –

'amend' includes repeal and apply (with or without modifications);

'the appropriate Minister' means the Minister of the Crown having charge of the appropriate authorised government department (within the meaning of the Crown Proceedings Act 1947);

'the Commission' means the European Commission of Human Rights;

'the Convention' means the Convention for the Protection of Human Rights and Fundamental Freedoms, agreed by the Council of Europe at Rome on 4th November 1950 as it has effect for the time being in relation to the United Kingdom;

'declaration of incompatibility' means a declaration under section 4;

'Minister of the Crown' has the same meaning as in the Ministers of the Crown Act 1975;

'Northern Ireland Minister' includes the First Minister and the deputy First Minister in Northern Ireland;

'primary legislation' means any –

  (a) public general Act;

  (b) local and personal Act;

  (c) private Act;

  (d) Measure of the Church Assembly;

  (e) Measure of the General Synod of the Church of England;

  (f) Order in Council –

    (i) made in exercise of Her Majesty's Royal Prerogative;

    (ii) made under section 38(1)(a) of the Northern Ireland Constitution Act 1973 or the corresponding provision of the Northern Ireland Act 1998; or

    (iii) amending an Act of a kind mentioned in paragraph (a), (b) or (c);

and includes an order or other instrument made under primary legislation (otherwise than by the National Assembly for Wales, a member of the Scottish Executive, a Northern Ireland Minister or a Northern Ireland department) to the extent to which it operates to bring one or more provisions of that legislation into force or amends any primary legislation;

'the First Protocol' means the protocol to the Convention agreed at Paris on 20th March 1952;

'the Sixth Protocol' means the protocol to the Convention agreed at Strasbourg on 28th April 1983;

'the Eleventh Protocol' means the protocol to the Convention (restructuring the control machinery established by the Convention) agreed at Strasbourg on 11th May 1994;

'remedial order' means an order under section 10;

'subordinate legislation' means any –

(a) Order in Council other than one –

(i) made in exercise of Her Majesty's Royal Prerogative;

(ii) made under section 38(1)(a) of the Northern Ireland Constitution Act 1973 or the corresponding provision of the Northern Ireland Act 1998; or

(iii) amending an Act of a kind mentioned in the definition of primary legislation;

(b) Act of the Scottish Parliament;

(c) Act of the Parliament of Northern Ireland;

(d) Measure of the Assembly established under section 1 of the Northern Ireland Assembly Act 1973;

(e) Act of the Northern Ireland Assembly;

(f) order, rules, regulations, scheme, warrant, byelaw or other instrument made under primary legislation (except to the extent to which it operates to bring one or more provisions of that legislation into force or amends any primary legislation);

(g) order, rules, regulations, scheme, warrant, byelaw or other instrument made under legislation mentioned in paragraph (b), (c), (d) or (e) or made under an Order in Council applying only to Northern Ireland;

(h) order, rules, regulations, scheme, warrant, byelaw or other instrument made by a member of the Scottish Executive, a Northern Ireland Minister or a Northern Ireland department in exercise of prerogative or other executive functions of Her Majesty which are exercisable by such a person on behalf of Her Majesty;

'transferred matters' has the same meaning as in the Northern Ireland Act 1998; and 'tribunal' means any tribunal in which legal proceedings may be brought.

(2) The references in paragraphs (b) and (c) of section 2(1) to Articles are to Articles of the Convention as they had effect immediately before the coming into force of the Eleventh Protocol.

(3) The reference in paragraph (d) of section 2(1) to Article 46 includes a reference to Articles 32 and 54 of the Convention as they had effect immediately before the coming into force of the Eleventh Protocol.

(4) The references in section 2(1) to a report or decision of the Commission or a decision of the Committee of Ministers include references to a report or decision made as provided by paragraphs 3, 4 and 6 of Article 5 of the Eleventh Protocol (transitional provisions).

(5) Any liability under the Army Act 1955, the Air Force Act 1955 or the Naval Discipline Act 1957 to suffer death for an offence is replaced by a liability to imprisonment for life or any less punishment authorised by those Acts; and those Acts shall accordingly have effect with the necessary modifications.

22 Short title, commencement, application and extent

(1) This Act may be cited as the Human Rights Act 1998.

(2) Sections 18, 20 and 21(5) and this section come into force on the passing of this Act.

(3) The other provisions of this Act come into force on such day as the Secretary of State may by order appoint; and different days may be appointed for different purposes.

(4) Paragraph (b) of subsection (1) of section 7 applies to proceedings brought by or at the instigation of a public authority whenever the act in question took place; but otherwise that subsection does not apply to an act taking place before the coming into force of that section.

(5) This Act binds the Crown.

(6) This Act extends to Northern Ireland.

(7) Section 21(5), so far as it relates to any provision contained in the Army Act 1955, the Air Force Act 1955 or the Naval Discipline Act 1957, extends to any place to which that provision extends.

Schedule I
The Articles
Part I
The Convention Rights and Freedoms
Article 2
Right to Life

1. Everyone's right to life shall be protected by law. No one shall be deprived of his life intentionally save in the execution of a sentence of a court following his conviction of a crime for which this penalty is provided by law.

2. Deprivation of life shall not be regarded as inflicted in contravention of this Article when it results from the use of force which is no more than absolutely necessary:

(a) in defence of any person from unlawful violence;

(b) in order to effect a lawful arrest or to prevent the escape of a person lawfully detained;

(c) in action lawfully taken for the purpose of quelling a riot or insurrection.

Article 3
Prohibition of Torture

No one shall be subjected to torture or to inhuman or degrading treatment or punishment.

Article 4
Prohibition of Slavery and Forced Labour

1. No one shall be held in slavery or servitude.

2. No one shall be required to perform forced or compulsory labour.

3. For the purpose of this Article the term 'forced or compulsory labour' shall not include:

(a) any work required to be done in the ordinary course of detention imposed according to the provisions of Article 5 of this Convention or during conditional release from such detention;

(b) any service of a military character or, in case of conscientious objectors in countries where they are recognised, service exacted instead of compulsory military service;

(c) any service exacted in case of an emergency or calamity threatening the life or well-being of the community;

(d) any work or service which forms part of normal civic obligations.

Article 5

Right to Liberty and Security

1. Everyone has the right to liberty and security of person. No one shall be deprived of his liberty save in the following cases and in accordance with a procedure prescribed by law:

(a) the lawful detention of a person after conviction by a competent court;

(b) the lawful arrest or detention of a person for non-compliance with the lawful order of a court or in order to secure the fulfilment of any obligation prescribed by law;

(c) the lawful arrest or detention of a person effected for the purpose of bringing him before the competent legal authority on reasonable suspicion of having committed an offence or when it is reasonably considered necessary to prevent his committing an offence or fleeing after having done so;

(d) the detention of a minor by lawful order for the purpose of educational supervision or his lawful detention for the purpose of bringing him before the competent legal authority;

(e) the lawful detention of persons for the prevention of the spreading of infectious diseases, of persons of unsound mind, alcoholics or drug addicts or vagrants;

(f) the lawful arrest or detention of a person to prevent his effecting an unauthorised entry into the country or of a person against whom action is being taken with a view to deportation or extradition.

2. Everyone who is arrested shall be informed promptly, in a language which he understands, of the reasons for his arrest and of any charge against him.

3. Everyone arrested or detained in accordance with the provisions of paragraph 1(c) of this Article shall be brought promptly before a judge or other officer authorised by law to exercise judicial power and shall be entitled to trial within a reasonable time or to release pending trial. Release may be conditioned by guarantees to appear for trial.

4. Everyone who is deprived of his liberty by arrest or detention shall be entitled to take proceedings by which the lawfulness of his detention shall

be decided speedily by a court and his release ordered if the detention is not lawful.

5. Everyone who has been the victim of arrest or detention in contravention of the provisions of this Article shall have an enforceable right to compensation.

Article 6

Right to a Fair Trial

1. In the determination of his civil rights and obligations or of any criminal charge against him, everyone is entitled to a fair and public hearing within a reasonable time by an independent and impartial tribunal established by law. Judgment shall be pronounced publicly but the press and public may be excluded from all or part of the trial in the interest of morals, public order or national security in a democratic society, where the interests of juveniles or the protection of the private life of the parties so require, or to the extent strictly necessary in the opinion of the court in special circumstances where publicity would prejudice the interests of justice.

2. Everyone charged with a criminal offence shall be presumed innocent until proved guilty according to law.

3. Everyone charged with a criminal offence has the following minimum rights:

(a) to be informed promptly, in a language which he understands and in detail, of the nature and cause of the accusation against him;

(b) to have adequate time and facilities for the preparation of his defence;

(c) to defend himself in person or through legal assistance of his own choosing or, if he has not sufficient means to pay for legal assistance, to be given it free when the interests of justice so require;

(d) to examine or have examined witnesses against him and to obtain the attendance and examination of witnesses on his behalf under the same conditions as witnesses against him;

(e) to have the free assistance of an interpreter if he cannot understand or speak the language used in court.

Article 7

No Punishment Without Law

1. No one shall be held guilty of any criminal offence on account of any act or omission which did not constitute a criminal offence under national or international law at the time when it was committed. Nor shall a heavier

penalty be imposed than the one that was applicable at the time the criminal offence was committed.

2. This Article shall not prejudice the trial and punishment of any person for any act or omission which, at the time when it was committed, was criminal according to the general principles of law recognised by civilised nations.

Article 8

Right to Respect for Private and Family Life

1. Everyone has the right to respect for his private and family life, his home and his correspondence.

2. There shall be no interference by a public authority with the exercise of this right except such as is in accordance with the law and is necessary in a democratic society in the interests of national security, public safety or the economic well-being of the country, for the prevention of disorder or crime, for the protection of health or morals, or for the protection of the rights and freedoms of others.

Article 9

Freedom of Thought, Conscience and Religion

1. Everyone has the right to freedom of thought, conscience and religion; this right includes freedom to change his religion or belief and freedom, either alone or in community with others and in public or private, to manifest his religion or belief, in worship, teaching, practice and observance.

2. Freedom to manifest one's religion or beliefs shall be subject only to such limitations as are prescribed by law and are necessary in a democratic society in the interests of public safety, for the protection of public order, health or morals, or for the protection of the rights and freedoms of others.

Article 10

Freedom of Expression

1. Everyone has the right to freedom of expression. This right shall include freedom to hold opinions and to receive and impart information and ideas without interference by public authority and regardless of frontiers. This Article shall not prevent States from requiring the licensing of broadcasting, television or cinema enterprises.

2. The exercise of these freedoms, since it carries with it duties and responsibilities, may be subject to such formalities, conditions, restrictions or penalties as are prescribed by law and are necessary in a democratic

society, in the interests of national security, territorial integrity or public safety, for the prevention of disorder or crime, for the protection of health or morals, for the protection of the reputation or rights of others, for preventing the disclosure of information received in confidence, or for maintaining the authority and impartiality of the judiciary.

Article 11

Freedom of Assembly and Association

1. Everyone has the right to freedom of peaceful assembly and to freedom of association with others, including the right to form and to join trade unions for the protection of his interests.

2. No restrictions shall be placed on the exercise of these rights other than such as are prescribed by law and are necessary in a democratic society in the interests of national security or public safety, for the prevention of disorder or crime, for the protection of health or morals or for the protection of the rights and freedoms of others. This Article shall not prevent the imposition of lawful restrictions on the exercise of these rights by members of the armed forces, of the police or of the administration of the State.

Article 12

Right to Marry

Men and women of marriageable age have the right to marry and to found a family, according to the national laws governing the exercise of this right.

Article 14

Prohibition of Discrimination

The enjoyment of the rights and freedoms set forth in this Convention shall be secured without discrimination on any ground such as sex, race, colour, language, religion, political or other opinion, national or social origin, association with a national minority, property, birth or other status.

Article 16

Restrictions on Political Activity of Aliens

Nothing in Articles 10, 11 and 14 shall be regarded as preventing the High Contracting Parties from imposing restrictions on the political activity of aliens.

Article 17
Prohibition of Abuse of Rights

Nothing in this Convention may be interpreted as implying for any State, group or person any right to engage in any activity or perform any act aimed at the destruction of any of the rights and freedoms set forth herein or at their limitation to a greater extent than is provided for in the Convention.

Article 18
Limitation on Use of Restrictions on Rights

The restrictions permitted under this Convention to the said rights and freedoms shall not be applied for any purpose other than those for which they have been prescribed.

Part II

The First Protocol
Article 1
Protection of Property

Every natural or legal person is entitled to the peaceful enjoyment of his possessions. No one shall be deprived of his possessions except in the public interest and subject to the conditions provided for by law and by the general principles of international law. The preceding provisions shall not, however, in any way impair the right of a State to enforce such laws as it deems necessary to control the use of property in accordance with the general interest or to secure the payment of taxes or other contributions or penalties.

Article 2
Right to Education

No person shall be denied the right to education. In the exercise of any functions which it assumes in relation to education and to teaching, the State shall respect the right of parents to ensure such education and teaching in conformity with their own religious and philosophical convictions.

Article 3
Right to Free Elections

The High Contracting Parties undertake to hold free elections at reasonable intervals by secret ballot, under conditions which will ensure the free expression of the opinion of the people in the choice of the legislature.

Part III

The Sixth Protocol

Article 1

Abolition of the Death Penalty

The death penalty shall be abolished. No one shall be condemned to such penalty or executed.

Article 2

Death Penalty in Time of War

A State may make provision in its law for the death penalty in respect of acts committed in time of war or of imminent threat of war; such penalty shall be applied only in the instances laid down in the law and in accordance with its provisions. The State shall communicate to the Secretary General of the Council of Europe the relevant provisions of that law.

Schedule 2

Remedial Orders

Orders

1. – (1) A remedial order may –

(a) contain such incidental, supplemental, consequential or transitional provision as the person making it considers appropriate;

(b) be made so as to have effect from a date earlier than that on which it is made;

(c) make provision for the delegation of specific functions;

(d) make different provision for different cases.

(2) The power conferred by sub-paragraph (1)(a) includes –

(a) power to amend primary legislation (including primary legislation other than that which contains the incompatible provision); and

(b) power to amend or revoke subordinate legislation (including subordinate legislation other than that which contains the incompatible provision).

(3) A remedial order may be made so as to have the same extent as the legislation which it affects.

(4) No person is to be guilty of an offence solely as a result of the retrospective effect of a remedial order.

Procedure

2. No remedial order may be made unless –

(a) a draft of the order has been approved by a resolution of each House of Parliament made after the end of the period of 60 days beginning with the day on which the draft was laid; or

(b) it is declared in the order that it appears to the person making it that, because of the urgency of the matter, it is necessary to make the order without a draft being so approved.

Orders laid in draft

3. – (1) No draft may be laid under paragraph 2(a) unless –

(a) the person proposing to make the order has laid before Parliament a document which contains a draft of the proposed order and the required information; and

(b) the period of 60 days, beginning with the day on which the document required by this sub-paragraph was laid, has ended.

(2) If representations have been made during that period, the draft laid under paragraph 2(a) must be accompanied by a statement containing –

(a) a summary of the representations; and

(b) if, as a result of the representations, the proposed order has been changed, details of the changes.

Urgent cases

4. – (1) If a remedial order ('the original order') is made without being approved in draft, the person making it must lay it before Parliament, accompanied by the required information, after it is made.

(2) If representations have been made during the period of 60 days beginning with the day on which the original order was made, the person making it must (after the end of that period) lay before Parliament a statement containing –

(a) a summary of the representations; and

(b) if, as a result of the representations, he considers it appropriate to make changes to the original order, details of the changes.

(3) If sub-paragraph (2)(b) applies, the person making the statement must –

(a) make a further remedial order replacing the original order; and

(b) lay the replacement order before Parliament.

(4) If, at the end of the period of 120 days beginning with the day on which the original order was made, a resolution has not been passed by each

House approving the original or replacement order, the order ceases to have effect (but without that affecting anything previously done under either order or the power to make a fresh remedial order).

Definitions

5. In this Schedule –

'representations' means representations about a remedial order (or proposed remedial order) made to the person making (or proposing to make) it and includes any relevant Parliamentary report or resolution; and

'required information' means –

(a) an explanation of the incompatibility which the order (or proposed order) seeks to remove, including particulars of the relevant declaration, finding or order; and

(b) a statement of the reasons for proceeding under section 10 and for making an order in those terms.

Calculating periods

6. In calculating any period for the purposes of this Schedule, no account is to be taken of any time during which –

(a) Parliament is dissolved or prorogued; or

(b) both Houses are adjourned for more than four days.

Schedule 3

Derogation and Reservation

Part I

Derogation

The 1988 notification

The United Kingdom Permanent Representative to the Council of Europe presents his compliments to the Secretary General of the Council, and has the honour to convey the following information in order to ensure compliance with the obligations of Her Majesty's Government in the United Kingdom under Article 15(3) of the Convention for the Protection of Human Rights and Fundamental Freedoms signed at Rome on 4 November 1950.

There have been in the United Kingdom in recent years campaigns of organised terrorism connected with the affairs of Northern Ireland which have manifested themselves in activities which have included repeated murder, attempted murder, maiming, intimidation and violent civil disturbance and in bombing and fire raising which have resulted in death, injury and widespread destruction of property. As a result, a public emergency within the meaning of Article 15(1) of the Convention exists in the United Kingdom.

The Government found it necessary in 1974 to introduce and since then, in cases concerning persons reasonably suspected of involvement in terrorism connected with the affairs of Northern Ireland, or of certain offences under the legislation, who have been detained for 48 hours, to exercise powers enabling further detention without charge, for periods of up to five days, on the authority of the Secretary of State. These powers are at present to be found in Section 12 of the Prevention of Terrorism (Temporary Provisions) Act 1984, Article 9 of the Prevention of Terrorism (Supplemental Temporary Provisions) Order 1984 and Article 10 of the Prevention of Terrorism (Supplemental Temporary Provisions) (Northern Ireland) Order 1984.

Section 12 of the Prevention of Terrorism (Temporary Provisions) Act 1984 provides for a person whom a constable has arrested on reasonable grounds of suspecting him to be guilty of an offence under Section 1, 9 or 10 of the Act, or to be or to have been involved in terrorism connected with the affairs of Northern Ireland, to be detained in right of the arrest for up to 48 hours and thereafter, where the Secretary of State extends the detention period, for up to a further five days. Section 12 substantially re-enacted Section 12 of the Prevention of Terrorism (Temporary Provisions) Act 1976 which, in turn, substantially re-enacted Section 7 of the Prevention of Terrorism (Temporary Provisions) Act 1974.

Article 10 of the Prevention of Terrorism (Supplemental Temporary Provisions) (Northern Ireland) Order 1984 (SI 1984/417) and Article 9 of the Prevention of Terrorism (Supplemental Temporary Provisions) Order 1984 (SI 1984/418) were both made under Sections 13 and 14 of and Schedule 3 to the 1984 Act and substantially re-enacted powers of detention in Orders made under the 1974 and 1976 Acts. A person who is being examined under Article 4 of either Order on his arrival in, or on seeking to leave, Northern Ireland or Great Britain for the purpose of determining whether he is or has been involved in terrorism connected with the affairs of Northern Ireland, or whether there are grounds for suspecting that he has committed an offence under Section 9 of the 1984 Act, may be detained under Article 9 or 10, as appropriate, pending the conclusion of his examination. The period of this examination may exceed 12 hours if an examining officer has reasonable grounds for suspecting him to be or to have been involved in acts of terrorism connected with the affairs of Northern Ireland.

Where such a person is detained under the said Article 9 or 10 he may be detained for up to 48 hours on the authority of an examining officer and thereafter, where the Secretary of State extends the detention period, for up to a further five days.

In its judgment of 29 November 1988 in the Case of *Brogan and Others*, the European Court of Human Rights held that there had been a violation of Article 5(3) in respect of each of the applicants, all of whom had been detained under Section 12 of the 1984 Act. The Court held that even the shortest of the four periods of detention concerned, namely four days and six hours, fell outside the constraints as to time permitted by the first part of Article 5(3). In addition, the Court held that there had been a violation of Article 5(5) in the case of each applicant.

Following this judgment, the Secretary of State for the Home Department informed Parliament on 6 December 1988 that, against the background of the terrorist campaign, and the over-riding need to bring terrorists to justice, the Government did not believe that the maximum period of detention should be reduced. He informed Parliament that the Government were examining the matter with a view to responding to the judgment. On 22 December 1988, the Secretary of State further informed Parliament that it remained the Government's wish, if it could be achieved, to find a judicial process under which extended detention might be reviewed and where appropriate authorised by a judge or other judicial officer. But a further period of reflection and consultation was necessary before the Government could bring forward a firm and final view.

Since the judgment of 29 November 1988 as well as previously, the Government have found it necessary to continue to exercise, in relation to terrorism connected with the affairs of Northern Ireland, the powers described above enabling further detention without charge for periods of up to 5 days, on the authority of the Secretary of State, to the extent strictly required by the exigencies of the situation to enable necessary enquiries and investigations properly to be completed in order to decide whether criminal proceedings should be instituted. To the extent that the exercise of these powers may be inconsistent with the obligations imposed by the Convention the Government has availed itself of the right of derogation conferred by Article 15(1) of the Convention and will continue to do so until further notice.

Dated 23 December 1988.

The 1989 notification

The United Kingdom Permanent Representative to the Council of Europe presents his compliments to the Secretary General of the Council, and has the honour to convey the following information.

In his communication to the Secretary General of 23 December 1988, reference was made to the introduction and exercise of certain powers under section 12 of the Prevention of Terrorism (Temporary Provisions) Act 1984, Article 9 of the Prevention of Terrorism (Supplemental Temporary Provisions) Order 1984 and Article 10 of the Prevention of Terrorism (Supplemental Temporary Provisions) (Northern Ireland) Order 1984.

These provisions have been replaced by section 14 of and paragraph 6 of Schedule 5 to the Prevention of Terrorism (Temporary Provisions) Act 1989, which make comparable provision. They came into force on 22 March 1989. A copy of these provisions is enclosed.

The United Kingdom Permanent Representative avails himself of this opportunity to renew to the Secretary General the assurance of his highest consideration.

23 March 1989.

Part II

Reservation

At the time of signing the present (First) Protocol, I declare that, in view of certain provisions of the Education Acts in the United Kingdom, the principle affirmed in the second sentence of Article 2 is accepted by the United Kingdom only so far as it is compatible with the provision of efficient instruction and training, and the avoidance of unreasonable public expenditure.

Dated 20 March 1952. Made by the United Kingdom Permanent Representative to the Council of Europe.

Schedule 4

Judicial Pensions

Duty to make orders about pensions

1. – (1) The appropriate Minister must by order make provision with respect to pensions payable to or in respect of any holder of a judicial office who serves as an ECHR judge.

(2) A pensions order must include such provision as the Minister making it considers is necessary to secure that –

151

(a) an ECHR judge who was, immediately before his appointment as an ECHR judge, a member of a judicial pension scheme is entitled to remain as a member of that scheme;

(b) the terms on which he remains a member of the scheme are those which would have been applicable had he not been appointed as an ECHR judge; and

(c) entitlement to benefits payable in accordance with the scheme continues to be determined as if, while serving as an ECHR judge, his salary was that which would (but for section 18(4)) have been payable to him in respect of his continuing service as the holder of his judicial office.

Contributions

2. A pensions order may, in particular, make provision –

(a) for any contributions which are payable by a person who remains a member of a scheme as a result of the order, and which would otherwise be payable by deduction from his salary, to be made otherwise than by deduction from his salary as an ECHR judge; and

(b) for such contributions to be collected in such manner as may be determined by the administrators of the scheme.

Amendments of other enactments

3. A pensions order may amend any provision of, or made under, a pensions Act in such manner and to such extent as the Minister making the order considers necessary or expedient to ensure the proper administration of any scheme to which it relates.

Definitions

4. In this Schedule –

'appropriate Minister' means –

(a) in relation to any judicial office whose jurisdiction is exercisable exclusively in relation to Scotland, the Secretary of State; and

(b) otherwise, the Lord Chancellor;

'ECHR judge' means the holder of a judicial office who is serving as a judge of the Court;

'judicial pension scheme' means a scheme established by and in accordance with a pensions Act;

'pensions Act' means –

(a) the County Courts Act (Northern Ireland) 1959;

(b) the Sheriffs' Pensions (Scotland) Act 1961;

(c) the Judicial Pensions Act 1981; or

(d) the Judicial Pensions and Retirement Act 1993; and

'pensions order' means an order made under paragraph 1.

Index

LAW IN PRACTICE SERIES

from

Old Bailey Press
The New Publishers for Practitioners

This text is part of the new and dynamic *Law in Practice Series*.

The series comprises a range of *Concise Texts* dealing with recent developments in key mainstream areas of legal practice and providing a pathway through some of the more complex areas of contemporary legal practice (eg residential tenancies, financial services).

The *Concise Texts* have a number of features which give them a dynamism relevant to contemporary practice including the following:

- Topical, relevant and up-to-date
- Written for practitioners
- Clear and direct writing style
- Evaluative commentary
- Authors with relevant practice experience
- Support materials for Holborn College CPD courses
- Time-efficient reading
- Outstanding value for money

Further, the *Law in Practice Series* includes a number of specialist texts on some of the fast-emerging areas of contemporary legal practice.

Full details of the series is set out below.

Concise Texts	ISBN	Price
Civil Litigation	1-85836-285-7	£6.95
Commercial Property	1-85836-283-0	£6.95
Conveyancing	1-85836-286-5	£6.95
Criminal Law and Procedure	1-85836-290-3	£6.95
Employment Law	1-85836-291-1	£6.95

Entertainments Licensing Law and Practice	1-85836-334-9	£9.95
European Union Law	1-85836-297-0	£6.95
Identifying Current Residential Tenancies	1-85836-288-1	£6.95
Introduction to Financial Services	1-85836-287-3	£6.95
Matrimonial and Child Care Law	1-85836-296-2	£6.95
Residential Tenancies	1-85836-086-2	£6.95
Small Private Companies	1-85836-292-X	£6.95
Taxation	1-85836-293-8	£6.95
The Civil Practitioner's Guide to the Human Rights Act 1998	1-85836-336-5	£9.95
Wills and Probate	1-85836-295-4	£6.95

Forthcoming Concise Texts	ISBN	Price
Reorganisation of Public and Private Company Share Capital	1-85836-348-9	£6.95

Other Titles	ISBN	Price
Practitioner's Handbook	1-85836-339-X	£54.95
Environmental Law Guide	1-85836-079-X	£26.95
EU Law Today	1-85836-271-7	£14.95
A Guide to the Trusts of Land and Appointment of Trustees Act 1996	1-85836-267-9	£12.95
Materials Sourcebook on Environmental Law	1-85836-077-3	£23.95
Research on the Net	1-85836-269-5	£19.95

To complete your order, please fill in the form below:

Books required	ISBN	Quantity	Price	Cost
		Postage		
		TOTAL		

For UK, add 10% postage and packing.
For Europe, add 15% postage and packing.

ORDERING

By telephone to: Mail Order at 0171 385 3377, with your credit card to hand

By fax to: 0171 381 3377 (giving your credit card details)

By post to: Old Bailey Press, 200 Greyhound Road, London W14 9RY

When ordering by post, please enclose full payment by cheque or banker's draft, or complete the credit card details below.

We aim to despatch your books within three working days of receiving your order.

Name

Address

Postcode   Telephone

Total value of order, including postage: £

I enclose a cheque/banker's draft for the above sum, or

Charge my ☐ Access/Mastercard ☐ Visa ☐ American Express

Card number ☐☐☐☐ ☐☐☐☐ ☐☐☐☐ ☐☐☐☐

Expiry date ☐☐☐☐

Signature: ....Date: ....